Dr Jessica Schleider, PhD or, a trained therapist and an le-session mental health interventions: brief, carefully constructed programmes that teach new ways of thinking, coping or relating to the self and others. To date, more than sixty trials from around the world have shown that, if constructed with care, even the briefest of therapeutic experiences can help people cope with problems from depression to anger to anxiety, and benefits can be lasting. In fact, it was Dr Schleider's own experience with mental illness – and the moment during treatment that sparked her journey towards recovery – that first convinced her that brief, meaningful experiences (including self-guided ones!) can spur long-term change. Drawing on decades of research on single-session interventions, interviews with leading psychotherapy experts and diverse personal narratives of mental illness recovery, this book will unpack how people with mental health needs can facilitate, seek out and learn from 'moments that matter' – and how improved understanding of brief therapeutic experiences may change the mental healthcare system for the better.

little treatments big effects

How to Build Meaningful Moments that Can Transform Your Mental Health

JESSICA SCHLEIDER

ROBINSON

First published in Great Britain in 2023 by Robinson

10 9 8 7 6 5 4 3 2 1

A CIP catalogue record for this book is available from the British Library.

ISBN: 978-1-47214-722-6

Typeset in Gentium by SX Composing DTP, Rayleigh, Essex

Printed and bound in Great Britain by Clays Ltd, Elcograf S.p.A

Papers used by Robinson are from well-managed forests
and other responsible sources.

Robinson
An imprint of
Little, Brown Book Group
Carmelite House
50 Victoria Embankment
London EC4Y 0DZ

An Hachette UK Company
www.hachette.co.uk
www.littlebrown.co.uk

For David, Penny and Mochi,
who make every moment matter to me.

Contents

Preface
By John Weisz, PhD

For three decades, I have worked with my students and colleagues on developing and testing interventions for mental health. These psychotherapies have been designed for use by clinicians, typically across many weekly sessions, and only after two to five days of training clinicians to use the treatment properly. I am in good company. That's what most of the documented mental health interventions – for young people and for adults – have looked like for the past five decades. In fact, hundreds of randomised clinical trials have been published reporting tests of psychotherapies like these. The tests have shown positive effects: recent meta-analysis of those clinical trials have shown that, on average, people who receive one of these treatments are likely to have a better outcome than people in a control group.

So the treatments do help, but concerns have arisen about whether these traditional in-person psychotherapies are reaching most of the people who need support. Many of those with genuine mental health needs cannot afford professional care. Many others will never be referred to a clinical professional, and those who are referred may be waitlisted for months, given the shortage of clinicians that is now evident in countries around the world. Even those fortunate enough to begin therapy with a clinician may not stay long; most psychotherapy protocols call for ten to twenty sessions, sometimes more, but most people who start therapy stay for far fewer sessions, and many stop after only one. To put it simply, we psychotherapy developers have not been very successful at developing treatments that meet the real-world needs of the many people whose mental health requires attention and support.

This concern took centre stage for Jessica Schleider and me when she was a graduate student in my lab at Harvard. We wondered whether there might be a simpler, more direct approach to mental health support that would be more accessible than traditional in-person therapy, and still produce measurable benefit. We took a special interest in the work of Carol Dweck, my fellow grad student at Yale many years before. Her work demonstrated very brief interventions teaching 'growth mindset' – the notion that personality, academic performance and personal outcomes can be changed if we treat setbacks as opportunities to grow and improve. It occurred to Jessica and me that growth mindset might also have beneficial effects for those who face mental health challenges and setbacks. That idea took root and eventually flowered in the form of a growth mindset intervention designed to help young people combat depression and anxiety. That intervention was compressed into a single session, based in part on a meta-analysis by Schleider and Weisz showing surprisingly strong benefits of single-session mental health interventions. Accessibility of the growth mindset intervention was magnified even more by making it entirely digital, consistent with increasing evidence showing that therapy delivered by devices can actually work well. The study testing this digital, single-session growth mindset intervention produced marked reductions in youth depression and anxiety symptoms over a period of nine months – quite remarkable for an intervention that young people complete in just half an hour, and in fact so remarkable that the article reporting the findings was judged the best paper of 2018 by the *Journal of Child Psychology and Psychiatry.* It is no exaggeration to say that this study dramatically upended traditional ideas about psychotherapy and what it must consist of to improve people's mental health. When it comes to really helping people, the study suggested, maybe less can be more.

The growth mindset study launched what has quickly become a stellar career, in which Jessica Schleider has shown, repeatedly, just how powerful brief, highly scalable interventions can be. Some of her interventions, now widely adopted throughout the US and in countries around the world, are entirely digital and are made widely accessible to all who need them if they only have internet access. Other applications of her ideas have changed prevailing notions of what *in-person* psychotherapy must be and how long it needs to take; it is possible, as she has shown, to make therapy with a clinician highly efficient by cutting to the chase – zooming in on the core problem and targeting steps to a solution. Working with a real clinician can make a difference for many, but it doesn't have to take months or years, as the Schleider approach has shown.

In this beautifully written book, we learn about a variety of ways little treatments can have big effects. We learn about many different ways this simple truth has been applied to the lives of real people in diverse circumstances, and about the beneficial effects on those lives. And we learn, touchingly, about the very personal relevance of this core idea to the author who shares with us the mental health challenges confronted and overcome as the adolescent Jessica matured to become the famous Professor Schleider. She is human, like the rest of us, and her humanity lends a glow to these pages, just as her wisdom does. Readers of this moving volume are in for a very special experience that may well enrich their lives.

Introduction: Why Little Treatments Matter to Me

Most meaningful moments are built on authenticity. In that spirit, I'd like to start this book by telling you why I wrote it. There are two stories. Both of them are true, and both are important to me, but one is much harder to tell.

First, the professional story (the easy one). As a clinical psychology PhD, trained therapist, and professor, I've spent over a decade studying and delivering mental healthcare – and growing convinced that most current treatment systems are built to fail. Psychological suffering is nothing new, and attempts to relieve it have cost billions over the last century. Yet rates of mental illness continue to rise worldwide. Most people with mental health needs get *no treatment at all.* And this gap is a feature, not a bug, of how care is delivered: for the most part, mental health treatment happens in brick-and-mortar, hard-to-access clinics; it's carried out by highly trained professionals, over very long periods of time (often, months to years). If the number of licensed therapists magically doubled overnight, provider shortages would *still* be insurmountable. Treatment would still be unaffordable, clinics out of reach, and insurance coverage unreliable. The process of finding a therapist would still resemble a labyrinth of pointless, unfunny riddles, with answers that shift by the day – perfectly constructed to deter those most desperate for help.

I wrote this book because a science-backed solution to increasing access to mental health support *already exists*, but most people don't know about it. Brief and single-session mental health interventions are supported by decades of international research and practice, including my own lab's work. These interventions are intentionally short, designed to fit into *one* therapeutic encounter; that is, they acknowledge the dual realities that any therapeutic experience might well be someone's last, and that it can be genuinely helpful anyway. These interventions are scalable, flexible and useful; some are therapist-led, others are self-guided. And I believe they can help fill gaps in treatment systems – quite literally, by being embedded into spaces where no other supports exist. I wrote this book because a more accessible, inclusive and hopeful approach to mental healthcare will stay impossible until people can imagine an alternative. Hopefully, this book makes that alternative not just imaginable, but actionable.

Second, the personal story. This one is harder to tell, but just as important. As an adult, I've built expertise around the gaps in mental healthcare systems. But I first encountered these gaps at the age of twelve, when my only research experience was a science fair project testing whether microwaves boost bean sprout growth (they don't).

I can't remember exactly when food, and (not) eating, overtook all of my waking thoughts – somewhere in between a classmate educating me on the calorie count of a Pop Tart, and falling prey to a deep sense of social inadequacy that typifies middle school for many. But when it happened, it was swift and severe. I needed help, and fast. My mother spent entire days on phone calls to eating disorder specialists, only to hear, 'Sorry, we're booked,' or 'How's six months from now?' on a loop. Even in New York City – known anecdotally for a near-comical surplus of therapists – affordable options were slim to none. My family's insurance covered nothing (this was 2002, well before mental healthcare parity laws were passed in the United States), and the cost of a single day in residential care equalled one month of rent in an NYC apartment. That my family found a therapist for me at all was miraculous – but I needed more intensive care than we could manage. Years with benign-but-insufficient treatment went by, and I did not recover. The eating disorder transformed our home into an angry, resentful space. When I was in high school, I developed suicidal thoughts, and I kept them to myself, desperate to avoid more family conflict – and knowing that, as a minor, I couldn't get help without parental permission. Barrier after barrier to mental healthcare cost me a decade of my life.

Altogether, I received hundreds of hours of treatment, and much of it blended together. But I'll never forget the moment when things began to change. After yet another lapse at the age of twenty-three, I self-enrolled in an intensive outpatient programme in Cambridge, Massachusetts, while working on my PhD (my student status gifted me the best health insurance I'd ever had). For two months, I attended three hours of treatment daily, including a supervised meal and two group skill-building sessions. After one of the meals, in my second week there, a fellow patient turned to me and asked, 'What made you try your fear food today?' (It had been years since I'd tried the food in question – something I'd mentioned in a prior group session. Technically, this sort of 'food talk' was verboten, but now I'm glad she broke the rule.)

'I'm not sure,' I said. 'I usually don't try harder foods until I feel ready. But I doubt that would've happened by itself. So I just did it.'

'Are you okay?'

I nodded yes.

She smiled. 'So, what if that's the *whole thing*?'

'Just doing hard stuff, instead of waiting to want to?' I asked.

'Right. What if you just woke up in the morning, and decided to eat something that's scary – but every day, even if you aren't sure you can, even if you are having a hard time, no matter what happened the day before?'

'Aha, sure,' I replied. Then, we had two group therapy sessions, about which I recall nothing. I was far too stuck on her comment.

It kept my mind busy for days. How could she think it was that simple? If just making daily choices about food were an option, wouldn't I have recovered by now? What about the years of history and negative thinking and family conflict, and the outlived functions my disorder continued to serve?

... Or what if I don't know who I am without an eating disorder, and unknown outcomes are scary, so I've never given daily, intentional, difficult choices an honest try?

My internal shift from impetuousness to vulnerability was striking, so I tried taking her advice. I treated each day as a clean-slate opportunity to make choices that directly opposed what my disordered thoughts told me to do, regardless of whether I'd 'succeeded' on the prior day. I started to show myself that my past experiences and present thoughts do not rob me of my capacity to act differently *today*. Unkind inner thoughts can be loud and upsetting, the past can feel insurmountable, and yet I can still take actions that feel hard at any given moment, because my long-term health and happiness depend on it. *I don't have to feel ready for recovery to take steps towards it.*

That unplanned interaction, and the realisations and actions it spurred, was a turning point in my trajectory toward health. To this day, staying well remains effortful, and better and worse days persist. But since that moment, I've come to know that working toward recovery is both within my control and worth it. By helping me reflect on my capacities in a new way, and giving me a mental means of decoupling my past experiences from my current actions, that moment *mattered* to me. Was it responsible for the entirety of my recovery? No. Could it have replaced other care I'd received? Also no. Would the same moment have been a 'turning point' for all others in my position? No – of course not. But for me, at that time, a single interaction *did* fill a critical gap in my own self-knowledge, which ultimately proved crucial to my progress.

And I believe it could have happened years earlier.

Research tells us that brief, therapeutic experiences like mine aren't always accidental. Similar experiences can be constructed: you can seek them out to facilitate new ways of understanding yourself and your world. These brief experiences cannot and should not replace other forms of treatment, just as mine did not. But people can *learn* to create them; providers can learn to offer them; and they can be *intentionally embedded* within and beyond ecosystems of care. Ideally, these moments could be created early in treatment (or even before treatment starts), to offer faster, potent support for those in acute need of help. This book will unpack why systemic change in mental healthcare is necessary; the science behind how brief interventions can make it possible; different types of meaningful moments that people have had, that scientists have studied, and that *you yourself* can construct; and an action-orientated path toward making it happen.

Finally, a note on whom this book is for. If you're still here, I wrote this book for you. Per population-wide studies, 80 per cent of people meet criteria for a mental illness at some point in their lifetimes. Even if you're in the lucky 20 per cent, odds are good that someone you care about is not. That person deserves easy-to-find, low-cost, science-backed support, if and when they need it – including tools they can benefit from right now, on their own. Broadly accessible brief interventions, or *moments that matter*, could help realise this possibility for you, your loved ones, and others without sufficient care. And I will try my best, in our brief and valuable time together, to show you how.

1

How Access Became an Afterthought in Mental Healthcare

'Now I understand that therapy has been around for ages. You wouldn't have known it, growing up in my community. It feels like the whole concept of mental health treatment wasn't made for people like me.'

– BL, aged twenty-seven, on seeking mental health treatment after growing up in a small, rural town in England

BL entered adulthood without once hearing the term 'anxiety disorder', despite his earliest childhood memories featuring fear, and little else. He can barely recall a time when he did not feel certain that something awful was about to happen – and that somehow, whatever it was, it would be all his fault. He was baffled by how seamlessly his grade-school peers talked and played together, apparently unbothered by the prospect of accidentally causing their families terrible harm. At the age of fourteen, as his fears grew larger and louder, BL worked up the courage to seek solace from his parents. Understanding and empathy would have been enough. But their response – 'it's mind over matter'; 'we just push through'; 'there are bigger fish to fry' – reminded him that, in his community, inner fears like his were seen as frivolous quibbles, not signs of illness warranting treatment. His rural hometown was small, tightknit and working class; mental health problems were understood as either defects requiring long-term hospitalisation (which BL did not), or as private issues to be conquered by sheer force of will. Either way, they were of little concern compared to his family's daily struggles to make ends meet. Treatment for BL's anxiety was not just unavailable; it was unknowable, inconceivable. It took ten years, leaving home, and discovering newfound social support for BL to seek formal treatment (and that process brought obstacles of its own, which we'll discuss shortly). But until then, his anxiety was never acknowledged – so it could never be addressed.

BL's story is shared by far too many. Today, amidst #ItsOkayNotToBeOkay social media campaigns and celebrity endorsements of the benefits of psychotherapy, mental health support *feels* like it should be accessible, at least for those who need it. Unfortunately, the roots of its inaccessibility run deep, built on historical stigma, fragmented systems, and chronic underfunding. That is, inaccessibility is literally embedded into mental health treatment today.

This chapter will explore some of the 'whys' behind the shortcomings of modern mental healthcare: why most people with mental health needs do not receive care, and why existing systems underlying this gap will keep reproducing themselves – unless we do something different. Unpacking the structure, stigmas and previously attempted fixes that drive modern-day mental healthcare can put current problems into context and highlight where new solutions are needed most.

And if you've struggled to access treatment of your own, I hope this chapter offers well-deserved validation, and a reality check. Trying and failing to access mental health treatment can be demoralising, and self-blame is common. You might have wondered if perhaps you are going about it the wrong way, or you don't deserve treatment, or you shouldn't have asked for help in the first place. Knowing why treatment is so out of reach will not make up for lost months or years spent searching, calling, waiting. But maybe, in some small way, it can help it all make sense.

You can stop wondering. It's not you. It's the (lack of a) system.

Accessibility was never the point

Access is easy to take for granted, unless and until it's gone. When I'm at home, I'm never thirsty, because the sink spouts clean water. My car's fuel tank is always fillable, thanks to the station down the street. I can walk without tripping from one end of my apartment to the other, because the lights reliably work. These things are true because when the city of New York was built, electric wiring, the sewage system and mobility were deemed social necessities. They were contemplated, embedded, updated and government-funded. And today, if my pipe bursts, or there's a fuel shortage, or a storm warps the electric grid, I can reasonably expect it to get fixed, fast. And life stays on hold until said fix is complete.

Access opens the world. Because you're sure that certain basics are going to stay met, you can plan, connect, create and engage beyond your in-the-moment needs. When it comes to electricity, water and mobility, the goal of accessibility – the idea that everyone should be able to get something when it's needed – is uncontroversial. In many parts of the world, these needs are still chronically unmet, but there is little debate that they *should* be, that lacking access is a problem, and that solutions call for major, structural investments – not just extra shovels for people to dig for groundwater.

Mental illness has existed for as long as humans have, but only in the past century has the concept of 'accessibility' been linked to mental health treatment. Unlike water, electricity and transportation systems, mental healthcare was never imagined as something for everyone. It was first built, and has largely stayed, as something meant for the othered, the damaged and the depraved – or, in many cases, something for the rich and the white. Concerns of accessibility have been superimposed on to mental healthcare's centuries-old roots, long after they had grown unjust. The state of mental health treatment today is the natural end result of relegating access to an afterthought.

Mental healthcare's access problems can be traced to the very bones of its design. Two specific design features have become especially sticky barriers to building a system that everyone can – and is meant to – benefit from: the problems of *vertical* and *horizontal* integration of mental health services.[1] (These terms have roots in the business world, but they've been recently repurposed for the healthcare sphere.) In a vertically integrated mental healthcare system, the level of support someone needs links up to the level of care that's immediately available to them; that level easily ratchets up or down as needs increase or decrease over time. Given vertical integration, a person experiencing a mental health crisis who improves within the first few days of hospitalisation would be seamlessly transferred to outpatient and community-based services once ready to leave the hospital; likewise, someone with just-emerging depressive symptoms would receive low-intensity outpatient support, to both alleviate their problems and stop them from getting worse.

The *horizontal* dimension refers to how well care is integrated across diverse health-related problems and settings – that is, the coupling of care for physical and mental health services. (Mental health supports housed in primary care clinics are a great example of 'horizontal integration'.) Given horizontal integration, someone reporting mental health needs to their primary care doctor would be quickly transferred to a care navigator or a therapist – depending on their symptoms, wants and needs. Failures in both vertical and horizontal integration of mental healthcare have rendered it virtually inaccessible to those in need of treatment, at the moments they need it most.

Vertical and horizontal disintegration are modern ways to describe mental healthcare's problems, but their roots are centuries old. They didn't happen by accident.

Asylums, deinstitutionalisation and the othering of mental healthcare

Step one to helping those with mental illness is not to harm them. For most of psychiatric treatment's history, despite good intentions, it is a step we've not come close to clearing.

The adage 'first, do no harm' is nothing new in medicine. The Hippocratic Oath is one of the oldest documents in human history; as early as the fourth century CE, it was carved on to physicians' tombstones, and it's now recited by newly minted medical doctors everywhere.[2] In taking it, physicians commit to providing care that centres patient autonomy (respecting the views, choices and actions of others), beneficence (acting to benefit others), non-maleficence (avoiding harm), and justice (treating people fairly). Early mental illness asylums, though born from progressive aspirations, evolved in total opposition to these ideals.* As historian Edward Shorter summarises in his *History of Psychiatry*, 'the rise of the asylum is the story of good intentions gone bad'.[3]

Starting in the nineteenth century, publicly regulated asylums were thought to represent a humane future for psychiatric care: a modern solution to the capricious, abusive conditions of the jails and 'madhouses' of centuries before. (London's Bethlem Royal Hospital, or 'Bedlam', is one notorious example, where passers-by could pay to watch mentally ill 'prisoners' for entertainment.)[4] That is, psychiatrists in the mid-1800s envisioned public asylums as curative, instead of custodial, by nature. As English psychiatrist and public asylum advocate Dr William Alexander Francis Browne wrote in 1837, 'the whole secret of the new [public asylum] system and of that moral treatment by which the number of cures has

* The history of psychiatric care is far older than nineteenth-century asylums, but government-funded asylums reflect the clearest predecessor to modern, government-funded approaches to treating mental illness as a medical problem. Earlier, mental health difficulties were largely addressed in the home, by families, or not at all.

been doubled may be summed up in two words, kindness and occupation' – referencing clinicians' compassionate care for patients through meaningful work.[5]

In 1845, the Lunacy Act of England and Wales upgraded the status of individuals with mental illness from 'criminals' and 'deviants' to 'patients' in need of care. This act led to the construction of asylums in every county, each of which required government inspections to ensure decent conditions. Together, these steps made nineteenth-century asylums the clearest predecessors to modern psychiatric hospitals. In France, officials passed an 1838 law to regulate asylum admissions and services across the country. In the United States, thanks to Dorothea Dix's advocacy against the horrid treatment of mentally ill people in jails, an 1842 law paved the way for the nation's first state-run asylum in Utica, New York.[6]

There was broad hope that making asylums official would lead to a higher quality of care for people with mental illness. What actually happened was the near-total opposite.

By the end of the nineteenth century, most industrialised nations had government-regulated asylums for people diagnosed with mental illness. (Often, these were people with psychosis, epilepsy, dementia or other forms of severe emotional dysregulation.) It also marked the start of the rapid unravelling of good intentions. As these asylums grew in number, so did their patient populations – but at a much faster rate than the institutions themselves. There are many proposed reasons for this increase, from patient 'redistribution' (e.g. shifting care responsibilities from families and jails to dedicated asylums), to population-wide increases in certain psychiatric conditions (alcoholic psychosis and neurosyphilis), to growing social recognition that mental illness could be treated at all. Causes notwithstanding, within a century, British and French asylum patient populations ballooned from a few hundred to hundreds of thousands. The mean number of patients in US asylums rose 927 per cent.[7] Without financial support for expansions and upgrades, overcrowding in asylums became the rule, not the exception. They rapidly devolved into the very custodial institutions they were meant to replace.

While more people were diagnosed as 'mentally ill' and sent away, funding continued to lag, oversight waned, and treatments drifted from ineffectual (pleasant conversations with kind attendants) to abusive (ice-cold baths, mechanical restraints and cycles of physical violence and neglect, used to subdue patients rather than treat them).[8, 9] And as asylum conditions worsened, psychiatrists' hopes for their curative potential collapsed – indeed, the goal of healing was abandoned entirely, dismissed as unrealistic for people admitted to asylums at all.[10] In turn, the function of asylums was solidified: they became state- and professionally sanctioned tools for the social and physical segregation of those with mental illness from the rest of society – more often than not, indefinitely. Regardless of good intentions, asylums served to crystallise public, medical and self-stigma for the patients they housed.

In her first-hand account *Ten Days in a Madhouse*,[8] investigative journalist Nellie Bly went undercover to document the true nature of the conditions in asylums. On assignment for *New York World*, she checked herself into a boarding house under a pseudonym, intent on feigning mental illness to gain admission to the Women's Lunatic Asylum on then-Blackwell's Island (modern-day Roosevelt Island). Within days, she had succeeded. By refusing to sleep, play-acting paranoia, and capitalising on social stigma against the mentally ill (as the boarding house's assistant matron shared, 'We do not keep crazy people here'), Bly raised enough suspicion about her mental state for other boarders to summon the police. From there, she was brought to a courthouse, deemed 'drugged' by a judge after pretending to suffer from amnesia, and assessed by several Bellevue Hospital psychiatrists, each of whom declared her 'positively demented . . . a hopeless case'.[8]

Hours later, she was admitted to Women's Lunatic Asylum. Her ten-day stay was more than enough to reveal its inhumanity. 'For crying the nurses beat me with a broom-handle and jumped on me,' one patient shared with Bly. Others were choked, beaten and berated by nursing and medical staff, offered stale or spoiled food ('I found a spider in my [slice of bread], so I did not eat it,' Bly wrote of her first asylum meal), and subjected to baths of dirty, ice-cold water ('hydrotherapy', allegedly to lessen agitation and mania) until they stopped struggling. Some would be left to drown.

Once she was admitted to the asylum, Bly abandoned her insanity act, instead acting as she typically would. But medical staff seemed wilfully blind to this shift. 'The more I endeavoured to assure [doctors and nurses] of my sanity,' Bly wrote, 'the more they doubted it.' An immutable 'mentally ill' identity, it seemed, had been assigned to Bly within moments of her admission. She believed that many other patients had suffered similar fates, with their distress and illness reflecting the asylum's conditions, rather than their true selves:

> What, excepting torture, would produce insanity quicker than this treatment? Here is a class of women sent to be cured. I would like the expert physicians who are condemning me for my action, which has proven their ability, to take a perfectly sane and healthy woman, shut her up and make her sit from 6 a.m. until 8 p.m. on straight-back benches, do not allow her to talk or move during these hours, give her no reading and let her know nothing of the world or its doings, give her bad food and harsh treatment, and see how long it will take to make her insane. Two months would make her a mental and physical wreck. [8]

Underfunding and overcrowding of asylums rendered them little more than patient warehouses: unliveable institutions that stigmatised the sick, and inevitably made them sicker. Because those admitted to asylums were rarely released, and without public awareness of treatment conditions, the rest of society could easily view asylum patients as incurable – or perhaps unworthy of trying to cure, given their presumed deficiencies. Plus, with people experiencing mental illness out of sight and out of mind, the entire issue of curability and treatment quality was easy for most to ignore.

By the early twentieth century, even psychiatrists (most of whom were employed within asylums) had sunk to a reputational low. Asylums and their doctors were denounced by colleagues in other specialties as unscientific and ineffective. As neurologist Weil Mitchell famously proclaimed at an annual neurology conference in 1894, 'Whatever the gullible public might believe about therapy, we [non-psychiatrist physicians] hold the reverse opinion, and think your hospitals are never to be used save as the last resource.'[11]

The asylum era ended with both patients and mental health professionals being othered, shunned and dismissed. It built figurative and literal wedges between people with mental illness and the rest of society, and between the treatment of mental illness and all other kinds of health. By stigmatising patients with mental illness as second-class humans and their doctors as second-class physicians, the asylum era effectively cut off hope for vertical and horizontal integration between existing mental health treatment and all other forms of care.

Deinstitutionalisation and its discontents

By the mid-twentieth century, the backlash against the failures of asylums – and against the segregation of psychiatric patients from general medical, vocational and community support – had reached a breaking point. This unrest gave way to the deinstitutionalisation movement, aimed at rebuilding community-based systems of mental healthcare.[12] In the United States, support for a new wave of community mental health clinics was authorised under the 1963 Community Mental Health Act: the first time in the country's history that federal funds were allocated to mental healthcare. Two years later, the creation of Medicaid underscored societal shifts from inpatient to outpatient mental healthcare (per a key piece of the Medicaid legislation, federal funds would not cover inpatient care in psychiatric hospitals). Across Europe, there were similar government-backed pushes to close or dramatically reduce asylum-based treatment, from Italy's 1978 Law 180 (which blocked all new admissions to public mental hospitals)[13] to the United Kingdom's 1959 Mental Health Act (which erased the distinction between psychiatric and non-psychiatric hospitals, and redirected mental health treatment to the community, where possible).[14] Similar reforms later took hold in Latin America via the 1990 Declaration of Caracas, which moved mental health treatment to primary care settings and mandated the deinstitutionalisation of individuals with severe mental illness.[15]

As in the asylum era, deinstitutionalisation efforts were launched by well-intentioned healthcare professionals, advocates and government officials, many of whom had noble, patient-centred goals. And, as in the asylum era, chronic underfunding, high needs and stigma made their dreams of community-based treatment impossible to realise.

Deinstitutionalisation outcomes were mixed, and they varied across countries. To be sure, fewer individuals in the United States were subjected to inhumane treatment in asylums. Likewise, in England, Germany, Italy, the Netherlands, Spain and Sweden, and soon after across seventeen Latin American countries, asylums were massively downsized or gradually closed altogether.[16] This was a solid start. However, the community-based and outpatient alternatives promised to patients never seemed to materialise. In many nations, there simply weren't enough outpatient clinics to meet demands for psychiatric care (a reality that remains true today). Further, many patients in the United States who truly *did* need inpatient support could no longer access it, thanks to Medicaid's new limits on the number of psychiatric inpatients that hospitals could serve. Some countries showed continued commitment to investing in community-based treatment options (for example, the UK has an impressive array of early-intervention teams and stepped care, thanks to government support). But across the globe, custodial placements for the mentally ill are *still happening*, every single day. For example, between 1990 and 2002, the number of psychiatric beds available fell substantially in England, Germany, Italy, the Netherlands and Spain – but involuntary psychiatric admissions *rose* in three of these five countries, and the prison population grew in all of them by 16–104 per cent.[17] From 1991 to 2017, the number of psychiatric beds available fell in Latin American countries by 35 per cent on average, while across them all, prison populations – with consistently high rates of mental health problems – *increased* by an average of 181 per cent.[18] After the US Community Mental Health Act, the number of asylum patients shrank from more than half a million in 1955 to fewer than 100,000 by the 1980s – yet from 1972 to 2009, the US prison population rose 700 per cent,[19] and up to 50 per cent of people incarcerated in the US today experience mental illness.[20]

Some argue that these figures show 're-institutionalisation': a shift of people with mental illness from one oppressive, custodial system (asylums) to another (prisons).[21] But this story doesn't quite fit. In the United States, most now-incarcerated people with mental illness would never have been treated in the psychiatric hospitals of the past. Asylum patients were mostly white and middle-aged, split equally across women and men; incarcerated people in the US today are mostly people of colour, young and male.[22] Likewise, in Latin America, the link between rising prison populations and fewer psychiatric beds is far from one-to-one.

In other words, even if post-deinstitutionalisation efforts to ramp up community care had succeeded, mass incarceration would still have led to a rise in custodial placements for people with mental illness. Today, we simply see a *different* state-sanctioned system for stigmatising and segregating a new sub-population of mentally ill people – while leaving those who *might* have been admitted to mid-century asylums in a desert of options for treatment.

And what about the people whose problems weren't severe enough for asylums, but who struggled nonetheless with debilitating anxiety, depression or distress? Perhaps you noticed that they've been absent from this narrative completely. After centuries of stigmatising, hiding and structurally devaluing mental health treatment for serious illness, a system for identifying and supporting the millions of people with moderate-but-still-impairing mental health problems simply never got built. We'll discuss the labyrinth of expenses, waiting lists, and inequities facing these folks – who reflect the majority of people seeking mental healthcare today – in the sections below.

From asylum-era abuses to deinstitutionalisation and the fragmented systems they yielded, one trend has stayed steady: the systematic and structural othering and de-prioritising of mental illness and its treatment, which persists across the globe.

This history sowed seeds for a treatment system where mental health problems were *actively and thoroughly isolated* from other forms of social and medical support, all but erasing any chance for vertical or horizontal integration of care.

So, what happens now to people who need help?

The last section began by stressing the importance of vertical mental healthcare integration (creating easy avenues for ratcheting people's mental health supports up or down, as needed) and horizontal integration (uniting mental healthcare and other types of medical care) to meet society-wide needs. As I write this book, true integration of mental health treatment along either axis remains theoretical. But many, many people still need help every day. So, what do they do? Who helps them, and how, and when? Answers vary, but together, their stories are stark reminders of the need for new pathways to accessing support.

When mental healthcare is chronically disintegrated and under-funded, those who need help anyway face several stark realities: crises become the quickest (or only) path to treatment; a two-tiered mental healthcare hierarchy prevails (especially in the United States, and, to a lesser degree, in other countries with insurance-reliant healthcare systems and stark wealth disparities); treatments based on scientific evidence are deprioritised, disincentivised and nearly impossible to get; and even the few who *do* access treatment are rarely able to complete it.

Reality one: Crises become the best (or only) route to support

In an integrated mental healthcare system, checkpoints and safety nets are built in. When you visit your primary care doctor for an annual check-up, they assess your mental health, just like your heart rate and blood pressure. If your psychological check-up flags you as 'at risk', you're referred to a specialist – maybe they're on site, and you see them right away, or perhaps you book an appointment elsewhere for the next day. They provide a brief, low-intensity treatment, or a more in-depth one if your symptoms are particularly troublesome, followed by a gradual tapering of support, until mental health goals are achieved. Your care is calibrated to your needs, precisely when and where they're first detected. And your health insurance pays for every part of it.

This set-up may sound reasonable, efficient and even cost-effective. Yet for many people, it couldn't reflect reality any less.

CL (aged twenty-four, from England) first felt the weight of major depression at the start of her second year at university. She watched, as though from outside herself, as her mood, motivation and energy melted away. Grades dropped, and emotions muted. Passing thoughts of self-harm evolved into concrete urges, and CL was scared. Based on family history, she knew her experience signalled a need for treatment. So she mustered her waning motivation and made an appointment with her primary care doctor, certain he'd know what to do.

Reality fell short of her hopes. 'I went to the doctor and said, "I'm really struggling, it's been a while, I don't think I'm going to get better." He didn't really understand . . . he was a [general practitioner], not trained in a mental health way. That was the first barrier, trying to get him to understand.'

So, CL persisted. She detailed her family's mental health history and listed the myriad ways in which her symptoms undermined her relationships, studies and day-to-day functioning. What she felt was beyond simple sadness, she explained. It was overwhelming nothingness, swallowing her will to fight back.

Her doctor offered sympathy, followed by a stark reality. 'Although he was compassionate and kind, he explained that there was no point in putting me on the waiting list [for mental health treatment], because by the time I finished university, I still wouldn't be at the top of it.'

It was then that CL's hope deflated. 'I remember thinking, *What's the point? No one's going to help me.*' The next week, she tried to access a therapist through her university's counselling service, 'but they were in the same position, oversubscribed, and it was a year's wait'. It was all too much. Eventually, giving into her symptoms seemed her only plausible option. Days and nights got hard to endure. The inner pain grew dull, constant and intolerable.

Eighteen months after her doctor's visit, CL attempted to end her life. Within hours, a crisis team intervened. CL was assessed, monitored for several days via home-based services, and ultimately paired with a support worker, who visited CL two to three times weekly. Finally, CL knew for sure that someone cared. All at once, she received the lifelines she'd needed for years.

'It's unfortunate that it had to get to a crisis point for me to receive any sort of care,' CL shared with me. 'But that was the only way to get to the top of the waiting list.'

Like too many others, CL endured predictable harms from a system lacking clear paths to early intervention: timely detection and treatment of psychiatric symptoms before they become unmanageable. There is no question that early intervention helps people stay engaged in school, work and relationships; it also improves long-term health, and reduces odds of experiencing poverty, homelessness, unemployment, suicidal thoughts and drug use. There is also no question that early intervention is necessary. Close to half of mental health conditions develop by age fourteen, and 75 per cent emerge by age twenty-four. Spotting and treating problems as soon as they arise keeps them from getting worse. It just makes sense. Frankly, the need for early mental health intervention is tough to argue against.

And yet, systems for early intervention scarcely exist. In a population-wide study in the United States, the average delay to accessing treatment after first noticing psychiatric symptoms was *more than a decade*, and earlier contact with non-psychiatric healthcare providers had no impact on whether (or how quickly) people accessed mental health support.[23] Mexican adults face similar delays, with average times to accessing treatment for substance use, mood disorders and anxiety disorders hovering at ten, fourteen and thirty years, respectively.[24] In Germany, teens wait an average of one to two years before receiving care after a suicide attempt.[25] English adults with bipolar disorder may wait up to 122 days after experiencing manic or depressive symptoms before accessing treatment – and only those needing immediate hospitalisation manage to get help faster.[26]

The list of unacceptable statistics goes on.

What happens to people once they do experience mental health crises varies by country, region and city. In much of the United States, due to long-standing underfunding of crisis services for mental health emergencies, law-enforcement officers tend to serve as de facto first-responders to crises. The consequences of this trend have been deadly. One in four fatal police shootings in the US between 2015 and 2020 involved a person with mental illness. Nearly 2 million US adults with mental illness are booked into the nation's jails each year, and up to 70 per cent of the 600,000 young people placed in juvenile detention centres annually have diagnosable mental illnesses.[27] Millions more young people and adults in psychiatric crisis end up diverted to emergency departments that are ill-equipped to address their needs. After involuntary admission, they sometimes wait days to see a mental health professional.[28]

Sometimes, and in certain places, post-crisis care has been (re)built to help. A few US states (including Arizona, Georgia and Tennessee) have piloted community-based mobile crisis teams, which deploy behavioural health specialists – rather than law-enforcement officers – to provide on-call early intervention to people in crisis.[29] (Unfortunately, the COVID-19 pandemic has severely cut state and local budgets for these kinds of programmes, preventing the systems from proliferating.)

For CL, in the UK, her treatment post-suicide attempt was precisely what she needed. Her professional crisis team monitored her until she was safe, checking in once every seventy-two hours; from there, her support worker followed up with her regularly for close to ten months. After her crisis point, care was swiftly calibrated to her needs.

A woman I interviewed from Spain shared a similar path to accessing treatment. When she first approached her primary care doctor about depression and suicidal thoughts, he suggested breathing exercises. It took six months of suffering and an attempt to end her life before she was involuntarily hospitalised and treated. But her recovery thereafter was supported by a solid, well-structured step-down system: 'When I was ready to leave the hospital, it was an easy transition. The hospital recommended a therapist, and when I moved, they again helped me find someone. I felt really cared for. The help they set up for me, the fact that they cared enough to keep helping, it really saved me.' The hospital's warm hand-offs, she said, reassured her that her struggles would not go ignored.

For both women, the contrast in care from pre- to post-crisis was striking. Months to years of nothing, and then, suddenly, everything. It hurts to wonder how their paths might have differed, had an integrated mental healthcare system caught and addressed their needs before they became dire.

It hurts to wonder how many paths have ended too soon, because no such systems exist.

Reality two: A two-tier mental healthcare system

Stigma-busting campaigns around mental illness often harp on familiar refrains – 'it's okay not to be okay'; 'you are not alone' – that crescendo to a common, confident message: *Reach out for help, and you will receive it.* Mental healthcare is just a phone call (or text, or email) away. Contact a local provider, just as you would for a shoulder injury or a stomach bug, and solutions will be within your reach. *There is no need to struggle in silence. At any moment, you can simply choose not to.*

This messaging all but guarantees frustration, confusion and a sense of defeat in those who actually do reach out for help – and for whom reaching out itself is *already* a Herculean feat, thanks to energy-depleting symptoms and distress. These help-seekers learn almost immediately that asking for and accessing care are not one and the same. They are barely related. Unless, of course, money is no object.

The underfunding and othering of mental health treatment has produced many harms, and our de facto two-tier treatment system is among its most pernicious (this is especially glaring in the US). Mental health treatment is not considered a human right, so its devaluation has evolved without recourse. Insurance coverage for treatment is variable, despite legal and policy efforts to establish parity; trained therapists who do accept insurance are overwhelmingly scarce; and in most cases, physical and mental healthcare systems remain worlds apart. As a result, psychotherapy is difficult to find and often too costly to pursue. In effect, it has become a luxury item – something nice for those who can afford it, but deemed superfluous and unnecessary to general health or survival.

The non-profit organisation Mental Health America releases nationally representative reports on the USA's 'State of Mental Health'. Data from 2021 show the population-wide impacts of America's two-tier treatment system. In that year alone, more than 27 million Americans with mental illness went untreated.[30] The number of people reporting unmet treatment needs has increased every year since 2011, with 56 per cent of US adults with mental illness receiving no treatment in 2021, and 73 per cent of youth with severe depression getting inconsistent care – or none at all. Adults and children alike lack adequate insurance coverage: 11.1 per cent of Americans with a mental illness are uninsured, a figure that has risen two years in a row, despite the passage of the Affordable Care Act, which was meant to improve equal coverage of physical and mental health needs. Furthermore, 8.1 per cent of youth – at least 950,000 children – had insurance that provided no mental health coverage at all. On a dramatic and worsening scale, modern mental healthcare systems, and that of the United States in particular, fail the very people who need them most.

These disparities do not reflect low demand or desire for mental health support. In a 2018 survey of US adults by the Cohen's Veterans Association and the National Council of Mental Wellbeing,[31] nearly 60 per cent surveyed were actively seeking (or wanted to seek) mental health services for themselves or a loved one. The barriers they faced were largely on the supply side of the equation: 42 per cent rated cost and poor insurance coverage as the top barriers for accessing mental health treatment. One in four people reported choosing between getting mental health treatment or paying for daily necessities, like rent and food, and one in five had to choose between getting treatment for a mental or a physical health condition. Other barriers to care were internal (and how could they not be, in a society that devalues mental healthcare as frivolous and unnecessary, while stigmatising and othering those who need higher-intensity treatment?). Close to one third of Americans worried about others judging them for seeking services, with 21 per cent saying that they had lied to avoid telling people about their treatment needs. Perhaps most damningly of all, 29 per cent of those who wanted to seek treatment for themselves or a loved one didn't know where to look for support.

Unsurprisingly, these access barriers aren't distributed at random. They are problems, almost exclusively, for the historically underserved. Compared to middle- and high-income households, low-income Americans are less likely to know where to go for mental health treatment – and so they are less likely to look. Of the Americans that did not seek mental health treatment (despite wanting or needing it) in 2018, more than half – 53 per cent – lived in low-income households.[31] People living in rural areas, compared to urban or suburban neighbourhoods, felt more stigma against treatment-seeking and had lower odds of pursuing needed care. And even when rural Americans do try to access speciality treatment, they often come up empty: more than half of US counties have no practising psychiatrists, 37 per cent have no psychologists, and two thirds have no psychiatric nurse practitioners – and all of these numbers are substantially higher in rural versus urban areas of the United States.[32, 33]

People of colour face added layers of discrimination and stigma, making treatment even more elusive. Hispanic Americans, Native Americans and Alaska Natives are two and a half times more likely than non-Hispanic white Americans to be uninsured – which on its own can make mental health treatment a financial impossibility.[34] And when Black Americans do reach out for support, they may be less likely than white Americans to receive calls back from providers. In a 2016 study, Heather Kugelmass (then a doctoral student at Princeton University) randomly chose 320 New York City psychotherapists listed in a popular insurance company's directory.[35] She then had voice actors leave voicemails for each of them, reporting depression and requesting an appointment. For their messages, the actors followed carefully constructed scripts that varied grammar, vocabulary and dialect to signal race and class (e.g. African-American vernacular or Black-accented English for African-American callers' scripts, and heavy New York City accents for low-income white callers' scripts). All callers reported the same symptoms, requested appointments at similar times, and noted having insurance that the therapists all accepted.

Kugelmass's findings were sobering. Only 17 per cent of African-American middle-class callers received a call back with any sort of appointment offer, compared to 28 per cent of white middle-class callers. And only 8 per cent of working-class callers received appointment offers, regardless of race. Gender differences intersected with race and class, painting a particularly stark picture for low-income Black men seeking treatment. Based on the study's results, an identifiably lower-income African-American man seeking therapy would need to call *sixteen times more therapists* than a middle-class white woman, just to be offered a first session.

Stories from the people behind these statistics bring treatment barriers into focus, from prohibitive costs to cultural stigma. RC, a twenty-two-year-old non-binary university student who had struggled (largely in silence) with obsessions and compulsions since childhood, recalled unspoken pressure to hide and dismiss their mental health needs: 'I was the only child of a minimum-wage working single mother. We barely had enough money for gas to get her to and from work and me to school, let alone for a psychologist or a psychiatrist, which provided an extra hurdle to jump over before I wanted to tell my mom what was going on with me.' Meanwhile, RC could scarcely sleep, thanks to paralysing fears that, if they did, their mother might be hurt or killed overnight.

MP, a twenty-seven-year-old woman living in the United States, shared a similar struggle over pursuing mental healthcare, despite clear and long-standing symptoms of post-traumatic stress disorder. 'Money was a big issue for me. The thought of paying a fee [US $35] each time for a session was really tough. I think growing up poor had a big influence on this. I didn't want to spend money on things unless it was absolutely necessary.' She paused after saying this, as though editing her thoughts in real time. 'But I know how silly this is, because taking care of your mental health is survival.'

Her thought struck me as anything but 'silly'. 'Reasonable, given broader healthcare and social systems that urge individuals to view physical health needs as legitimate but mental health needs as frivolous' – that felt far more correct. But it's a mouthful to say, and in my experience, dismissing one's dilemmas as simple misperceptions is easier than grappling with systemic stigma.

When cultural stigmas meet the structural decoupling of medical and mental health support, barriers become even harder to navigate. In addition to cost concerns, MP noted how her family's background and beliefs shaped her delaying treatment as an adult. '[Growing up], I didn't know I needed mental healthcare . . . it didn't occur to me that I could even seek help. I think my culture plays a big part in this. Mental healthcare is not sought out in Asian communities. No one in my family talks about the issues they have . . . We see mental health difficulties as a demon potentially "latching on", and [believe] that these things go away through prayer or natural remedies.' For MP, the Americanised othering of mental illness compounded with cultural taboos and traditions, creating an especially cruel obstacle course of personal, familial and structural barriers to seeking help.

By the time MP did find her way into therapy, she had secretly managed trauma symptoms for nearly half her life. And still, she is among the lucky tier of people with treatment needs who make it to their first session at all.

* * *

America's two-tier mental healthcare system is no secret to those with power to fix it. The United States government has enacted policies meant to undo the 'luxurysation' of psychological care – namely, laws to increase 'insurance parity' for mental and medical treatment. Since 2008, United States health insurance companies have been *legally mandated* to provide the same coverage for mental healthcare as they do for physical healthcare. The Mental Health Parity and Addiction Equality Act (MHPAEA) is a federal law requiring Medicaid and commercial health insurance plans to impose the same financial requirements (e.g. fees per visit) and limitations (e.g. caps on session duration) on both physical and psychological treatment. No distinction at all is permitted between the insurance coverage for physical and mental health treatment. At least, in theory.

And 'theory' is what this law seems to remain. Six years after the MHPAEA went into effect, a survey by the American Psychological Association revealed that 96 per cent of Americans had no idea that the law existed – and only 7 per cent had ever heard the term 'mental health parity' at all.[36] Without knowing that a law exists, service users have no way of knowing when it's broken. As a natural result, enforcement of the MHPAEA has been abysmal. Remarkably few insurance companies are held accountable for repeated violations. In January 2022, the US Departments of Labor, Health and Human Services, and the Treasury released a damning fifty-four-page report to Congress detailing broad, persistent failures of health insurers and plans to provide equitable mental healthcare benefits to those they cover.[37] As one example of coverage failures (out of too many to list), one insurer provided coverage for nutritional counselling as part of a treatment plan for diabetes, but that same coverage was denied as part of a treatment plan for eating disorders (anorexia or bulimia nervosa).

This instance hits close to home. Early in my own treatment for anorexia, nutritional counselling was arguably *more* crucial to my recovery than was psychotherapy. It was a nutritionist – not a therapist – who crafted my first roadmap (an hour-by-hour meal plan) toward repairing a dangerous relationship with food.

Those sessions helped save my life. Then and now, insurance companies slot them as 'extra'.

Sometimes, where federal US laws fail, state-specific laws can bridge gaps and mend omissions. But state laws around mental health parity are just as poorly enforced as federal ones. In 2019, the Kennedy-Satcher Centre for Mental Health Equity co-led a report to evaluate the strength and quality of individual states' mental health and addiction parity statutes.[38] The report identified an avalanche of deficiencies in state parity laws across the country: forty-three of fifty US states received a final grade for mental health parity of 'D' or 'F'. The report concluded: 'For many individuals directly impacted by mental illness or substance use disorders, the promise of parity remains elusive. They are denied care when they need it most and have few resources to advocate on their own behalf.'[38]

The recent reports on federal and state mental health parity failures both call for greater enforcement of existing parity laws. Certainly, this would help – but parity enforcement on its own is no quick fix. Even when people with insurance coverage *do* manage to book their first therapy session, it's unlikely to be with a provider that accepts insurance at all. Thanks partly to long-standing underfunding of mental healthcare, insurance companies rarely compensate clinicians at rates that reach a living wage, making it virtually impossible for them to both accept patients' insurance and also earn a living. As a consequence, psychiatrists are far less likely than other providers to accept any type of insurance: while 73 per cent of other providers accept Medicaid, only 43 per cent of psychiatrists do.[39] And slightly more than half of psychiatrists accept Medicare and private insurance, compared with more than 86 per cent of other providers.

Low reimbursement rates are only part of the reason why therapists end up 'out-of-network' more often than other types of healthcare providers. One US-based clinical psychologist, Dr Mary Alvord – a practising therapist for more than forty years who founded a non-profit dedicated to improving treatment access – shared how insurance companies ultimately forced her group practice entirely out-of-network, starting in around the mid-1980s: 'Not only did [the insurance companies] start to reimburse at lower rates, but they made up impossible rules. For example, one [company] said that if a claim wasn't received within thirty or sixty days [of a session], it wouldn't be paid at all! . . . After I suspected a pattern that they didn't receive many claims, I began to inquire of other practitioners. Behold, theirs too were "lost" in the mail. So, it's not only the rate of reimbursement [that's a problem], but the "rules" they make up.'

She went on to describe how often insurance companies' employees – individuals with no clinical training or experience – would challenge her claims on shaky (or non-existent) grounds: 'I once had to make a fifteen-minute appointment with [an insurance company] representative to review an MMPI [a well-established clinical personality assessment] that they rejected. The guy asked me questions that led me to believe he had no training. I told him, "You're asking basic questions, what was your degree in?" Not psychology. He wouldn't be allowed to administer an MMPI.' And yet he had full authority to deem her use of one as clinically unnecessary.

And so, Dr Alvord's practice converted to being entirely out-of-network. 'We would have to hire a full-time administrator just to handle the insurance company claims, and [we would all] get paid less – and with delays – if we took insurance at all.' And, as many well-trained therapists might tell you, it's tough to support others without the resources you need to support yourself.

All of this highlights at least two important points. First, ensuring mental health parity won't fix access to care, as long as practising therapists are structurally prevented from actually accepting insurance. Second, the problem of low treatment access is *not* due to individual therapists' supposed 'profit motives' (a refrain I've heard more than once from patients struggling to find treatment). Speaking as a trained therapist myself, most therapists I've met are genuinely motivated to help as many people with mental health needs as possible, to the best of their abilities and training. If it were realistic for them to accept insurance without going bankrupt – and without trading hours of treating patients for days of jumping through administrative hoops built by insurance executives with no clinical expertise – they would. Access-to-care problems didn't start with therapists, and given their scope, individual therapists alone can't solve them, either.

A thirty-eight-year-old American woman I interviewed summarised this mess elegantly, when recalling her months-long treatment-seeking saga for generalised anxiety, social anxiety and panic attacks: 'Finding a mental health provider that takes your insurance, and is accepting new clients, is an act of God.' Of course, it shouldn't be. But unless and until we achieve broad-scale health insurance overhaul, there's an urgent need to get creative about how, where and from whom people in need can quickly and reliably access help.

Reality three: Even people who access treatment aren't always helped

By definition, the success of efforts to improve access to treatment are judged by whether more people actually receive support – and if so, how many. Unfortunately, this definition misses a distressing reality within mental healthcare systems worldwide: 'accessing care' does not guarantee 'receiving treatment that *helps*'. This distinction between *getting treatment at all* and *getting treatment likely to work* has a name among academic psychologists: the 'research–practice gap'. This phrase captures the persistent reality that, despite decades of research and major advancements in identifying scientifically supported psychotherapies, most mental health treatments that patients receive are *not* those that science shows can help. And the research–practice gap makes treatment accessibility problems infinitely more complex to solve.

So, among the small subset of people lucky enough to access treatment at all, what do they actually get? In a 2004 World Health Organization survey of 60,000 adults in fourteen countries across the Americas, Europe, the Middle East, Africa and Asia, 'receiving mental health services' was defined as having one or more contacts with a provider of *any kind*, as long as that contact related to emotions, nerves, mental health, or drug or alcohol use.[40] Providers could be licensed professionals (psychologists or psychiatrists), general medical doctors (paediatricians or family medicine specialists), other healthcare providers (occupational or physical therapists), religious counsellors (a rabbi, minister or sheik), traditional healers, or peer counsellors. The definition of 'mental health services' varied widely from one country to the next, depending on local context. This reality provides a sobering backdrop for other treatment-access statistics: when we hear that only 20 per cent of people with mental health needs access support, 'support' could mean almost anything – from a months-long hospital stay to a single encounter with someone who's had little to no mental health training.

Other useful data come from the United States' National Comorbidity Survey-Replication study.[41] More than 9,000 people with psychiatric disorders answered questions about their recent mental healthcare, including the provider(s) they saw and the type and duration of treatment they received. The researchers defined 'minimally adequate treatment' as some sort of intervention (such as psychotherapy or medication), delivered over the course of more than one encounter, in a manner following evidence-based guidelines for the person's psychiatric disorder. With this more stringent (and evidence-informed) definition of 'minimally adequate treatment', the scope of the research–practice gap grew crystal clear. Across the entire sample, only 32.7 per cent of people with a psychiatric disorder received 'minimally adequate treatment' – suggesting that, at best, only one third of treatments provided to people with mental health needs met minimal standards of adequacy. 'Complementary' or 'alternative' mental health treatments accounted for 31.3 per cent of all mental health visits – despite the absence of scientific evidence suggesting their utility.

All in all, resolving the 'access to mental healthcare' problem isn't just a matter of improving people's access to *any* support. It's about improving people's access to support that *has some promise of actually helping them.*

If evidence-based mental health treatments exist, why aren't they regularly provided? The dominant model of providing mental healthcare – and in turn, the dominant structure of most evidence-based interventions – are often-named culprits.[42] In practice, once-weekly psychotherapy – delivered by an individual provider to an individual patient – is the dominant, if not 'default' support available to service users across the globe. In the past several decades, as research on mental health interventions has grown, virtually all new psychotherapies – including those tested in formal trials – have been built to fit this model. That is, a majority of 'evidence-based interventions' for mental health problems follow a predictable structure: they involve between twelve and twenty weekly, individual appointments, delivered via fifty-minute, face-to-face visits by a highly trained professional. Unfortunately, the 'once-weekly, fifty-minute therapy hour' model of care dramatically limits the degree to which treatment can extend to those with mental health needs.[43] For one, there simply *aren't enough trained providers* for a one-to-one, in-person, multi-session therapy model to serve population-scale needs. In the United States (an upper-income country), the number of trained mental health professionals is approximately 700,000 for a population of nearly 330,000,000.[44] Most of those 700,000 are located in upper-income, highly populated cities (versus rural regions of the country), and disproportionately few are trained to treat underserved populations, such as low-income people, people with minoritised identities, young children, people with disabilities and the elderly. In lower- and middle-income countries, the therapist shortage is even starker. For instance, there are 0.30 psychiatrists for every 100,000 people living in India.[45]

Even if the number of professional therapists were to miraculously double overnight, the total would still fall short of global needs – and the distribution of those therapists would boost treatment access only for those likeliest to already have it. Paired with barriers already discussed (like stigma, high treatment cost and unpredictable insurance coverage), creating 'evidence-based treatments' that require three to four months of individual weekly visits with a highly trained professional seems out of touch at best.

Another major reason why evidence-based mental health interventions are seldom used in real-world settings is that they weren't built to fit where, how and to whom treatment is delivered in practice.[46] With frustratingly few exceptions, these treatments were built without therapist or patient input, and in total isolation from on-the-ground systems of care.[47, 48] For many years, the working assumption in mental health treatment research has remained: 'If we build it (an effective mental health intervention), they will come (patients will access them).' This assumption has been proven exquisitely wrong.[46, 49, 50] In fact, it has led to several problems with existing evidence-based treatments that preclude their use beyond the research studies that validated them.

First, most evidence-based mental health treatments are 'focal interventions'. That is, they are designed to address just one specific disorder or problem type (e.g. one protocol for obsessive-compulsive disorder, another for depression, another for social anxiety).[51] There is certainly a time and a place for such interventions, and they do help a subset of patients – but their practicality is limited on several fronts. For example, 'focal treatments' are seldom an ideal match for real-world service users, because co-occurrence of multiple problems is the *norm*, not the exception.[41, 52] If a patient presents with co-occurring depression, substance use and anxiety, but each 'evidence-based treatment' targets only one of these domains, how is a therapist to select just one protocol, addressing only one of the issues at hand? Should they be expected to learn three separate twenty-session treatment protocols, and deliver them in parallel – or in sequence? None of these options are feasible or practical, and so many therapists opt for a more bespoke approach to providing therapy, based on clinical intuition and patients' in-the-moment needs. Unfortunately, the effectiveness of these bespoke approaches is often unknown and unmeasured.

Second, due to myriad structural and logistical barriers, most people who begin treatment cannot remain in treatment for the full, evidence-based 'dose'. Designing and validating treatments to last twenty weeks when the mean number of sessions is approximately four[53] directly undermines the practicality of evidence-based treatments in real-world practice settings. In fact, in an overwhelming number of cases, people are incredibly likely to access just *one* session of treatment with a professional of any kind – a statistic backed by a long list of sources and studies. To name just a few: in a multi-year evaluation of 115,000

Australian patients seeking community-based mental health support, 42 per cent attended just one session.[54] In a national sample of US adolescents, nearly 25 per cent of teens who accessed mental healthcare attended just one or two sessions before discontinuing.[55] Another study found that 20–57 per cent of psychotherapy 'drop-outs' occur after the first session,[56] and this figure rises to 60–70 per cent if we include 'drop-outs' that occur after session two.[57, 58] Similar mental health service use patterns have been documented in Canada,[59] Mexico,[60] Japan[61] and Spain.[62] These realities underscore the fact that existing mental health treatments were built to fit an imagined version of real-world mental healthcare – not for the true structure and dose of support that people actually receive.

Third, most evidence-based treatments were developed and validated by scientists, in university settings, and without much (or any) formal input from service users themselves.[48] (The importance of input from patients and service users has relatively recently been acknowledged by mental health funding agencies and treatment developers).[47, 48] Is it truly possible to build interventions that service users will want, accept, complete and benefit from, without once consulting the people those treatments are meant to serve? Psychology and psychiatry have histories of dismissing or side-stepping patient experiences and perspectives, and the 'gold-standard' pipelines for building and testing interventions – including the pipelines backed by federal scientific funding agencies across the globe – are no exception. The status-quo approach for identifying evidence-based treatments rarely includes the perspectives of people living with mental illness. This omission makes blind spots in the content, focus and structure of evidence-based interventions inevitable. Patients' perspectives on what they need, what helps, and how change happens are rarely built into the therapies available to them.

Some researchers have put in the work to learn from service users about their preferences and ideas for the treatment they want most. [48, 63, 64] From this research – and from my interviews and conversations with dozens of service users for this book – several needs are clear. Patients want solutions they can access right away, in their moments of need, without months-long waits and before they reach crisis points. They want to feel understood, listened to, respected and cared for by those delivering care. They want flexibility in where, how quickly, in what form and for how long (or how briefly) they can access services. Some want long-term services, and others want briefer supports, accessed as and when they are needed. They want options beyond traditional, provider-delivered treatment, such as peer-led or self-guided programmes – including options housed outside formal treatment systems, which can be hard to navigate and even harder to trust (especially for patients with negative prior treatment experiences). They want solutions that promote their autonomy rather than take it away. None of these wants or needs are unreasonable, yet they are rarely centred in how treatments are developed. And they certainly don't shape whether a treatment is deemed 'evidence-based'.

Just as BL shared of his struggles seeking mental healthcare in his small, English town: 'It feels like the whole concept of mental health treatment wasn't made for people like me.' The truth in his perspective is hard to overstate, and it highlights an important reality: to improve the scale and accessibility of effective mental health support, past approaches to building, testing, and disseminating interventions will never suffice.

Chapter conclusion

Too many people who need mental health treatment cannot access effective support. If you are or have ever been among those people (as I have), I hope this first chapter has clarified why – objectively and assuredly – *this was never your fault.* Mental healthcare systems across the globe have been built to fall short of population-wide needs for myriad, interconnected reasons, including:

1. Centuries of stigma and othering, baked into systems of mental health treatment, have only been reified by government underfunding.

2. There is a total lack of horizontal integration (e.g. uniting physical and mental health services) and vertical integration (e.g. helping patients shift from one level of treatment intensity to another), which has yielded fragmented and hard-to-navigate systems of care that leave many without support at all.

3. Thanks to underinvestment in mental health treatment, separation of private and public mental

health systems, insufficient insurance coverage and provider shortages, we have been left with a two-tier system of mental healthcare, meaning that treatment is broadly unavailable except to the most privileged segments of society.

4. Even among those who do access care, the effectiveness of that care is hard to predict – largely because evidence-based treatments were never designed to fit real-world systems or realities of care.

5. When considering solutions and building new interventions, service users have rarely been consulted, all but guaranteeing that these interventions will miss key needs of those they are meant to serve.

So, where do we go from here? Are there *any* promising paths toward helping you, and those you care for, access timely, effective mental health support, short of total overhauls of healthcare systems, insurance coverage and social attitudes toward mental illness? Overhauls will certainly be useful as long-term goals, but people are suffering now. And we can only start from where we are. As a first step, it seems necessary to consider creative solutions that minimise or challenge stigma; are easily embedded within cash- and resource-strapped care systems; are evidence-based *and* fit within current systems of care; may be accessed outside of formal treatment systems, so that people who would otherwise access *nothing* might instead access *something* with potential to help; and respond to the needs, experiences and priorities of service users themselves.

This 'first-step' set of solutions might feel just as overwhelming as the problems outlined in this chapter. Frankly, it could be, especially if imagined and approached all at once. But small, thoughtful steps are the critical building blocks for large-scale change. I hope you'll stick with me to consider how to make more accessible mental health supports our new normal. Equipped with solutions already known to help, that new normal may be closer and more attainable than it seems.

2

How Little Treatments Can Impact Mental Health

> 'What is the next right thing? How can I get one foot in front of the next? That, doing the next right thing, that was huge . . . [I started] solving the needs of the day. It's really simple stuff. And faithfully practised – that's the change agent.'
>
> – MW, aged sixty-six, on a realisation that helped him pursue recovery after years of unsuccessful treatment for drug use, alcohol use and mental illness.

I promise things get more hopeful from here.

The first chapter highlighted some of the key reasons why existing therapeutic supports have grown to be – and will likely remain – inaccessible and unaffordable to most, including baked-in stigma, lack of insurance coverage, provider shortages, insufficient partnership with service users, and the poor fit of existing evidence-supported psychotherapies to real-world settings.

In the spirit of transparency, writing Chapter 1 gave me a stomach ache. There is so much work to do. It can feel overwhelming. Ultimately, a better mental healthcare ecosystem will require long-term reinvestment in mental health, renewed societal valuing of therapists (and more therapists in general), and robust paths to insurance parity, at a minimum. But these solutions are long-term ones, by nature. They involve large-scale, slow-moving policy shifts and roll-outs, and even if implemented, they wouldn't boost treatment access or care integration anytime soon. They would fall woefully short of addressing the reality that there are, and will remain, many people who have access to *no support at all*, with no viable options on the horizon.

All of these problems are entrenched, severe, and long-standing. And, as must be acknowledged, they have all worsened dramatically in the context of the COVID-19 pandemic. At its onset in the early months of 2020, the pandemic disrupted or halted critical mental health services in 93 per cent of countries worldwide. Since then, we have faced constellations of fear, financial distress, social isolation, illness and grief – all of which have only accelerated the demand for mental health support. Before the pandemic, the mental health treatment gap was *already* unacceptably large. The unprecedented collective adversity caused by COVID-19 has widened it to alarming proportions, with professional and governmental bodies in the United States, the European Union and the United Kingdom declaring 'crises' and 'national emergencies' in mental health. Circumstances are extreme, and solutions at all levels are necessary.

So, when considering solutions, let's start small. Literally, with the smallest treatments possible.

Why little treatments, if the problems are so big?

It's a reasonable question to ask. To me, the most compelling answer is that people need help *now*. Historical stigma and structural inequities help explain why mental health treatment is broadly inaccessible. But pursuing policy-level fixes for those problems – aimed at improving social attitudes toward mental illness, expanding therapist training pipelines and increasing pay, and enforcing insurance parity in ways that stick – cannot help individuals who are struggling today, with no safeguards in sight. When it comes to 'top-down' versus 'bottom-up' solutions to our mental health crisis, it's a both–and, not an either–or. The remainder of this book will focus on a 'bottom-up' approach: what can we do *today* that will promote mental health in an accessible, patient-centred way, and that will continue benefiting people *before*, *while* and *after* top-down policy change is ongoing?

To start considering answers, I decided to consult service users directly. In the summer of 2021, I posted a call on Twitter for volunteers with lived mental illness experience to share 'turning points' in their recovery journeys (a concept we'll return to later), along with their experiences seeking treatment more broadly.[65] Within a week, I received ninety-eight survey responses from people living in eight different countries across North America, Europe and the United Kingdom: sixty-eight women, twenty-two men, and nine transgender or gender-diverse individuals, of whom 53 per cent were white/Non-Hispanic, 18 per cent were Asian, 2 per cent were Middle Eastern/North African, 6 per cent were Black, 8 per cent were multiracial, and 12 per cent were Hispanic/Latine. They were between eighteen and sixty-six years of age. In response to the survey question, 'Have you ever had trouble getting mental healthcare when you wanted it?' nearly 80 per cent selected 'Yes', in line with estimates from multi-national research. When those 80 per cent were further asked, 'What kept you from getting mental healthcare when you needed it?', their typed responses were remarkably consistent:

- Nearly three quarters (72 per cent) cited finances as a key access barrier.
- Two thirds (66 per cent) mentioned long waiting lists or a dearth of immediately accessible support.
- Half (50 per cent) endorsed fears of disclosure or worries about stigma.
- More than a quarter (26 per cent) cited a lack of autonomy and agency to pursue the sort of treatment they preferred (e.g. self-help rather than professional counselling; psychotherapy rather than medication; 'as-needed' sessions as opposed to once-weekly therapy).
- Approximately 8 per cent cited a lack of time to seek out support.
- Another 8 per cent were unsure where or how to look for treatment at all.

While this survey does not include a globally representative sample, participants' responses echo the access barriers most commonly cited in large-scale research studies.[66, 67] Collectively, they highlight several features that mental healthcare solutions should possess, to optimise their odds of overcoming the accessibility challenges that service users face. Best-fit solutions must be *readily available at moments of need*, as opposed to weeks or months after needs emerge – and well before individuals are in crisis. They must be *empowering* of service users' autonomy and preferences for different modalities of support. They must be *minimally stigmatising*, including programmes situated outside of formal healthcare systems and supports that do not require psychiatric diagnoses to receive. And they must be *affordable*, regardless of personal wealth.

These features – *available, empowering, non-stigmatising, affordable* – echo core principles of ethical healthcare more broadly (beneficence, autonomy, non-malfeasance, justice). In other words, service users are citing an unmet need for mental health treatment that satisfies even *basic standards of ethical care*. We need to capitalise on all available tools to address this need, as swiftly and broadly as possible.

Single-session interventions might offer an ideal toolkit for realising this goal.

What are single-session interventions?

Single-session interventions (SSIs) are nothing new. Successful one-session bouts of psychotherapy have been reported since the era of Freud.[68, 69] But the concept of *intentional* or *planned* single-session mental health intervention was first formally articulated by Moshe Talmon in his book *Single Session Therapy: Maximizing the Effect of the First (and Often Only) Therapeutic Encounter*: 'Single-session therapy is defined . . . as one face-to-face meeting between a therapist and patient with no previous or subsequent sessions within one year.'[70]

My research group has since expanded this early definition, using a similar lens to Talmon's, but including delivery models made possible by technological advances (e.g. digital, self-administered programmes that do not involve a trained therapist). In this vein, we offer an updated definition of SSIs as 'specific, structured programmes that intentionally involve just one visit or encounter with a clinic, provider or programme'.[71]

Intentionality in SSIs is essential. For example, early dropout from weekly therapy would not constitute an SSI, nor would an unplanned, ad hoc encounter with a healthcare professional. It's also notable that SSIs do not require any specific *type* or *style* of therapy (although single-session approaches do share common assumptions and principles; we'll return to these on page 84). The skills, strategies and focus of a given SSI can vary substantially, and SSIs can flexibly address *many* different problems – from anxiety and trauma to depression to relationship challenges. The 'service user' in the context of an SSI could be an individual adult or child, a family, a couple or a group; and the sessions may occur in an office, a hospital or a school – or at home, online, in the case of digitally mediated programmes. So, SSIs reference the intentional delivery of some single-encounter programmes, not a specific strategy, approach or treatment setting.

Another key facet of SSIs is their flexibility to be accessed 'one at a time' in an as-needed fashion. In other words, clients are empowered to seek out SSIs when and where they perceive needs for support – with *any individual SSI* holding the potential to spur positive, clinically meaningful change. This set-up provides the opportunity for any given SSI to be sufficient, while also leaving the door open for future care and support. So, one individual might access an SSI just once and feel that their needs have been addressed; another might seek out a few SSIs, perhaps across several months at moments of distress. There is no expected length for treatment. There are no missed sessions. Only singular, stand-alone opportunities to create positive change. This concept is elegantly stated by Rosenbaum,[72] one of the co-originators of therapist-delivered single-session therapy: 'Psychotherapy is not long or short . . . [it] depends instead on "good moments" where something profound shifts for a client.' Helping people craft their own 'good moments' is what SSIs are designed to do best.

With this context, we can delve into where the SSI concept came from; the evidence suggesting that they work; why they make sense as a means of expanding access to care, given systemic constraints and clients' wants and needs; and precisely how they might effect positive change. This will include deeper dives into SSI research and delivery models across North America, Europe and Africa, including my own lab's research on digital SSIs for teens.

At this point in the book, you may be feeling some degree of scepticism. Personally, speaking as a scientist, I think that's a good thing. The very concept of SSIs challenges leading assumptions of what treatment can and should look like. Norms of 'once-weekly therapy' and of defining 'brief interventions' as those that span three to four months (not one session!) are baked into mental health research and practice. Indeed, the notion that *any* clinical change can occur in a single session – especially for clients with complex, co-occurring problems – still strikes many professionals as far-fetched. (When I was a graduate student, after giving one of my first public talks on SSIs at an academic conference, a senior professor urged me to 'find myself a back-up research programme' for when my SSI work fell flat. Thankfully, I did not listen.) This wariness makes perfect sense. SSIs are still unfamiliar to most people, and any patient-facing innovation *should* be subject to close scrutiny before being rolled out at scale. Premature dissemination of unhelpful programmes benefits no one and may harm many.

That said, taking stock of thirty-plus years of SSI research, practice and creative applications – combined with my own scientific research on SSIs – has helped me reach a clear conclusion. I believe that systematically disseminating evidence-grounded SSIs could complement and extend existing mental healthcare systems, increase access to patient-centred, in-the-moment support, and overcome some of the treatment-access barriers that plague service-seekers most. SSIs can narrow gaps in mental healthcare ecosystems that standard psychotherapies cannot and will never fill.

My goal for the rest of this chapter will be to help you understand how I got here.

How did SSIs come to be?

There are reports of effective single-session therapies as early as the early twentieth century. They have been overviewed thoroughly by others (e.g. Cannistra and Piccirilli),[73] but I'll briefly summarise them here. A particularly striking example of an early SSI is that of Martin Grotjahn,[74] who successfully delivered a 'single-session treatment' in the 1940s to a patient with depressive symptoms. He wrote about his treatment approach, including the coping strategies discussed with his patient and how he adopted an active role as a clinician, in *Psychoanalytic Therapy: Principles and Application*.[75] Notably, at that time, the idea of single-session therapy was deeply countercultural – the psychiatric equivalent of sacrilege. Here is Cannistra and Piccirilli's translation of what Dr Seymour Saraon, Professor Emeritus of Psychology at Yale, noted in his autobiography regarding the response among psychiatrists to Grotjahn's account:

> He said that, under certain conditions, certain people with certain problems can, relatively quickly (sometimes in a single session), experience important and lasting changes, which somehow escape the theory. This . . . was as disconcerting to the community of analysts, professionals, and theorists as if the Pope had announced his conversation to Islam or his consent to abortion.[76]

But Grotjahn was not alone in his assertion that clinical change could occur quickly. Also in 1946,[76] Franz Alexander introduced the concept of a 'corrective emotional experience' – a within-person change resulting from a single, meaningful interaction or event. Corrective experiences may, but need not, occur within a patient–therapist relationship. Regardless of where they unfold, they entail moments when an individual 'understands or experiences . . . an event or relationship in a different and unexpected way', spurring newfound understandings of themselves or their circumstances.[77] As an example, imagine you disclose a personal detail, something you've experienced as shameful, to a family member. You anticipate judgement and rejection – but instead, they respond with warmth and support. In this 'corrective' moment, you might realise that your expectation of universal rejection, based on disclosing this personal detail, might be less accurate than you assumed. This realisation, in turn, might help you share more about yourself with others in your life, with a reduced sense of anxiety and shame. Since 1946, Alexander's suggestion that a single experience can catalyse meaningful change has remained central to clinical research on how psychotherapy effects change.[78]

Work led in London by David Malan may be viewed as the first formal evaluation of a single-session mental health treatment.[78] The authors report on the outcomes for forty-five patients described as first presenting for treatment with significant, long-standing psychiatric distress. All forty-five had completed a lengthy intake interview, but they missed their second appointment and then never returned. Malan and colleagues then followed up with these patients several years later, and observed that 51 per cent of their sample was deemed substantially symptomatically improved. Malan commented:

> Clearly, psychiatrists who undertake consultations should not automatically assign patients to long-term psychotherapy or even brief psychotherapy, but should be aware of the possibility that a single dynamic interview may be all that is needed. Finally, dynamically oriented psychiatrists should

> also be aware of the powerful potential therapeutic effects both of telling a patient that he must take responsibility for his own life, and of reassuring him that he can manage without therapeutic help.

Certainly, Malan's examination was not a rigorous study or controlled clinical trial. Nonetheless, his words represented a marked shift in field-wide beliefs about how change can happen. Not only does he suggest that *change within a single clinical encounter is possible*, but he specifically emphasises his view that *empowering patients* to draw on their own strengths and capabilities may itself be therapeutic.

In the decades that followed, 'brief therapies' received increasing attention from researchers and practitioners – and also from insurance companies, which were less and less willing to pay for multi-year intensive psychoanalysis. Short-term therapies drawing not just on psychoanalytic traditions, but on behaviourism and cognitive theories, started to spread across the globe,[79] paving the way for more rigorous tests of whether, and how, any individual therapy session can promote meaningful clinical change.

The first formal investigation of single-session intervention was led by Dr Moshe Talmon, with colleagues Dr Bob Rosenbaum and Dr Michael Hoyt, beginning in the mid-1980s. Talmon led several studies of single-session treatments through a partnership with Kaiser Permanente, a large healthcare organisation in California. They retrospectively reviewed the charts of 200 patients who had – for any reason – attended just one session of therapy before ending treatment. The researchers found that many of these patients had been 'very satisfied' with their single session of therapy, and as such, they did not feel the need to continue. Talmon's interest was piqued; along with his colleagues, he decided to study this 'single-session therapy' phenomenon in a new set of patients, aged from eight to eighty, presenting with widely ranging clinical problems. In this new trial, patients were told at the beginning of their first session that, although more sessions would be available to them, the therapist's goal would be to see whether just one session could accommodate their needs. That is, client choice was centred from the start: continuing and stopping after the first session were posed as equally acceptable options.

As reported in a series of published articles,[80, 81, 82] the researchers' results confirmed and extended their observations of past clients' charts. More than half of the fifty-eight clients (58.6 per cent) chose to conclude their psychotherapy after just one session, even though additional sessions were offered to them. Nearly 90 per cent of the clients who chose to receive a single-session intervention reported significant improvements in the 'presenting complaints' that led them to therapy, with 65 per cent reporting improvements in other key areas of functioning (e.g. peer or family relationships). And – to Talmon and his colleagues' surprise – follow-up interviews held three and thirteen months later revealed *no detectable differences* in treatment satisfaction or outcome scores between clients who opted to end treatment after one session, and those who continued for multiple sessions. One session – for some people, when empowered to choose for themselves – appeared to be enough.

Since this early work, studies have continued to suggest that more treatment is not necessarily better, and that single-session therapies might (for some) create lasting and meaningful change. For example, written exposure therapy, a treatment for post-traumatic stress that involves recalling, processing and making meaning of past traumatic experiences via timed sessions of expressive personal writing, produces substantial reductions in post-traumatic stress symptoms after just *three hours* of treatment – and it works just as well as multi-session, multi-month alternative post-traumatic stress disorder (PTSD) treatments.[83] Critically, written exposure therapy has higher completion rates than multi-session alternatives (94 per cent versus 61 per cent), so it might also be a more *realistic* option for those in need. Based on a systematic review of fifty-eight clinical trials, interventions lasting less than five minutes appear to have similar impacts on the alcohol use of young adults as multi-session interventions.[84] And several RCTs (randomised controlled trials – the 'gold-standard' treatment design), where clients were randomly assigned to receive *more* versus *fewer* sessions for treating phobias,[85] panic attacks,[86] insomnia,[87] post-traumatic stress,[88] and substance use,[89] have consistently revealed *no scientific support* for the superiority of longer, more intensive treatments. In short, the findings of Talmon and his colleagues appear to hold up. 'More is better' may not apply when it comes to mental health treatment. Of course, this is not to say that 'less is better', either; just that, in some cases, people may benefit similarly from 'more' or 'less' – to the extent that offering *both*, and allowing people to choose whether 'more' or 'less' best fits their own needs, is an option well worth considering.

The IAPT case for low-intensity mental healthcare

The idea that less treatment might (for some) be enough is perhaps best illustrated by England's Improving Access to Psychological Therapies (IAPT) initiative. IAPT was first introduced as England's new model for mental healthcare in 2007, based on the notion that many patients receiving evidence-based psychological therapy would likely never recover and return to work, massively exacerbating societal and economic burdens of mental illness.[90] Within a decade, there were over 200 IAPT services across England, representing the largest publicly funded example of evidence-based psychotherapy implementation in the world. IAPT has served as a model for the development of similar systems in other countries, including Australia,[91] Canada,[92] Norway,[93] Spain[94] and Japan.[95] The IAPT mental healthcare system has three key features: the use of evidence-based interventions; assessment of patient outcomes as a part of standard treatment; and a stepped-care model, where patients can access progressively intensive interventions according to personal need. More specifically, most IAPT patients are first offered a programme called 'guided self-help' (GSH): a brief, low-intensity treatment based on cognitive behavioural therapy, deliverable either by phone or online, and in groups or one-to-one. GSH in IAPT is delivered by a unique workforce of psychological wellbeing practitioners (PWPs), who are specifically trained (via a post-graduate certificate programme) to provide low-intensity interventions. (No comparable workforce exists in the United States, where all mental health providers must obtain *at least* a master's degree in order to practise independently.) IAPT patients who do not benefit from GSH are 'stepped up' to higher-intensity forms of therapy, which is offered by providers with more advanced training (e.g. clinical psychologists or psychiatrists). Since 2012, more than 5 million people in England have received some form of mental health treatment through IAPT.

IAPT's outcomes show precisely what can happen, on a national scale, when brief, low-intensity therapies become widely accessible to people seeking care. In a 2021 review of sixty studies of IAPT, including data from over 600,000 patients, patients showed large overall improvements in depression and anxiety, along with moderate improvements in work engagement and social adjustment.[96] Crucially, when low- and high-intensity IAPT interventions were compared, *patients showed largely equal benefits.* Declines in anxiety, functioning and depression *did not differ* for people who received low- versus high-intensity care. (For context, around 36 per cent of IAPT patients who attend more than one session receive only low-intensity interventions, 28 per cent only receive high-intensity interventions, and 34 per cent receive both; overall, the average number of sessions among patients who attend more than one IAPT appointment is 6.4.)[97] This result further affirms that, for a substantial portion of people, less-intensive mental health treatment really *can* be enough – or, at least, no better or worse than costly, high-intensity therapies that were never designed to scale.

Even with its many strengths, IAPT has not proven to be a panacea. First, up to 50 per cent of patients who receive IAPT services do not recover[97] – a percentage that is virtually identical to primary care-based mental health services pre-dating

IAPT's emergence.[97] Some have suggested that this comparison calls IAPT's added value into question. Second, even at its massive scale, IAPT *still* falls short of meeting population-level need: even today, it only meets around 16 per cent of need linked to depression and anxiety in England's community.[98] Third, existing evaluations of IAPT's effectiveness only include patients who attend two or more sessions of treatment - despite up to 47 per cent of patients attending just *one*.[99] These gaps confirm that other - perhaps even *more* scalable - approaches to mental health support remain needed to address population-level mental health.

Despite this need, and the large number of IAPT patients attending just one therapy session, SSIs have not been formally integrated into IAPT's structure. I spoke with Christopher O'Rourke, an IAPT PWP who delivers low-intensity interventions to older teens and adults of all ages, to learn more about why this might be the case.

'Single-session interventions are not yet encouraged or supported by NICE [National Institute for Health and Care Excellence] guidelines,' he explained, 'likely due to the relative newness of SSIs.' (In fact, SSIs have a history more than three decades long - but, in most circles, that history remains largely unknown, even to mental health professionals!) Since PWPs are expected to be fully 'NICE-compliant', any interventions excluded from those guidelines - even those with an international evidence base - are discouraged. But Christopher went on to stress: 'I definitely think [SSIs] should at least be trialled and researched within IAPT.' Despite the cost-effectiveness of a stepped-care model, he has observed that it 'does inadvertently facilitate patients dropping out of treatment'. Indeed, he has noticed that 'many of my patients at low intensity reach recovery quite early in the treatment pathway', so '[SSIs] would increase access to beneficial treatment, especially for patients who have many commitments, or have shift work and cannot commit to the same timeslot for a session every week or every fortnight'. For patients who *did* opt to continue treatment after an initial SSI, Christopher suggested that their early SSI could be supplemented with 'a review session, or guided self-help, or Step 3 [high-intensity] interventions, depending on their needs'. He viewed SSIs as a natural adjunct to the system that already exists – but one that has not been applied in any formal fashion.

Because SSIs are not yet included in IAPT, studies of IAPT cannot speak to the potential benefits of single-session approaches, only low-intensity and stepped-care models more broadly. So, how can we know whether SSIs *specifically* can spark clinical change, when implemented widely, at the population level? Following Talmon's early research, many additional studies – easily in the hundreds, including dozens of RCTs, with populations around the world – have tested whether SSIs can improve mental health. Taken together, they affirm SSIs as a positive force for promoting mental health at scale.

But before we dive into the science, I'd like us to get on the same page regarding what exactly it *means* to say that an SSI 'works'. It's a tricky term, but an important one to pin down, because it guides my understanding of SSI research to date.

What does it mean to say an SSI 'works'?

For some health conditions, knowing whether a treatment works is easy. After taking antibiotics for ten days, a patient with strep throat is typically cured of the condition, with no remaining physical signs of illness. But a treatment that 'works' does not always mean a 'cure', especially in the context of mental health. In a book chapter he describes as his 'final chapter on the subject of single-session therapy' (following dozens of chapters and books written over more than thirty years, and forty-two years of delivering single-session therapy to patients), Talmon shared his personal take on 'cures' in mental health treatment:

> The more I got devoted and committed to seeking psychohealth instead of psychopathology, resources over deficiencies, strengths and abilities over disabilities and disorders, the less convinced I got about the concept of 'cure' as a goal in psychotherapy. Most people (including myself) continue to be challenged by difficult and at times traumatic life events. In some cases, my own clients met life challenges by themselves and at other times returned for one or a few sessions as necessary . . . The pathogenic-medical model that therapy should start when a patient is properly diagnosed as being ill or having a mental disorder and should end when that patient is cured is, at best, misleading both for therapists and patients.[100]

To put it another way: humans lead challenging, complicated lives. Support needs will wax and wane with time. Indeed, many people who experience mental illness report fluctuations in their symptoms, largely due to shifting contexts and stress. So it may be unreasonable to expect *any* sort of mental health treatment – long or short – to totally, permanently 'cure' a person's mental health challenges, because their life circumstances will always continue to change. Research backs up the idea that even longer-term psychotherapy is unlikely to 'cure' patients in the long term. In a study of 502 RCTs of multi-session youth psychotherapy, treatments were found to have statistical 'upper limits' to their impacts on symptoms: 'Even with a therapy of perfect quality, achieved effect sizes may be modest.'[101] So, Talmon prefers an 'as-needed' approach to mental health support – and, in particular, to delivering intentionally single-session interventions. SSIs might be made accessible *precisely when a person perceives the need* – whether or not they've received a psychiatric diagnosis – with the acknowledgement that additional SSIs (or other forms of support) may be useful, for different reasons, at different points in life.

SSIs are not antibiotics. When they 'work', they may not 'cure' mental illness. But they can help make difficult emotions, thoughts or circumstances meaningfully easier to navigate. They can help your journey from this moment to the next feel less painful, and more fulfilling, than it would have otherwise. For some, the 'good moment' an SSI creates may provide a roadmap for addressing similar difficulties in the future, or spark new understandings that support better coping overall. And, if and when a new and overwhelming stressor emerges, the option of further support always remains available. In other words, SSIs help people *manage* their mental health problems, as and when they naturally unfold. They can 'work' whether or not a cure happens to occur.

Still, the question remains: if we can't measure whether an SSI has 'worked' based on the presence or absence of a diagnosis, what metrics should we use instead? Here, I find it useful to consider two different definitions of a treatment 'working', both commonly used in mental health treatment research. First, a treatment might 'work' (or not) in terms of reducing the *severity* of mental health-related problems that someone experiences (e.g. they may experience a shift from moderate to mild levels of depression symptoms, or from high to moderate levels of hopelessness). But just as importantly, a treatment might also 'work' (or not) in terms of meeting clients' perceived needs and fitting into their lives. Treatment researchers call the first definition *clinical effectiveness*, and the second *treatment acceptability*. Any intervention can 'work' in one, both or neither domain. For example, a treatment might 'work' in terms of reducing mental health problems, while also being near-impossible for clients to access, afford or complete (e.g. a $10,000 six-month treatment programme requiring two in-person sessions each week). Ultimately, for SSIs to be considered strong candidates for large-scale roll-out, they must be clinically effective *and* acceptable to the people they aim to serve. Otherwise, they are unlikely to fulfil their potential to narrow treatment-access gaps.

So, with this frame in mind, what does the science say about whether SSIs 'work' – both in terms of improving mental health, and meeting patients' needs?

Can SSIs improve mental health?

First, we can consider research on whether or not SSIs 'work' when it comes to reducing the severity of mental health-related problems. Indeed, evidence from RCTs suggests that they can. SSIs have decreased alcohol consumption among individuals with alcohol use disorder, across a series of trials including hundreds of adults;[102] they have increased distress tolerance and use of positive parenting practices, in a trial with 301 high-anxiety parents of young children;[103] they have reduced self-hatred and increased intentions to stop self-harming in a study of 565 teens with histories of non-suicidal self-injury;[104, 105] and they have produced clinically significant improvements in pain intensity in a study of 263 adults with chronic lower back pain, with the SSI performing just as well as an eight-session cognitive behavioural therapy (CBT) programme.[106]

In another RCT with 659 teens and young adults, an SSI using techniques from motivational interviewing led to reductions in adolescents' depression symptoms three months later, compared to receiving a list of local resources.[107] In a separate RCT with 100 clinically anxious parents, a group-based SSI for the parents helped prevent anxiety in their children: children with parents in the control group were 16.5 per cent more likely than those whose parents received the SSI to have diagnosable anxiety disorders at a follow-up one year later.[108] In yet another RCT with 216 Australian children and adolescents, youths with widely varying diagnoses (including ADHD, anxiety disorders, disruptive behavioural disorders and adjustment disorders) were randomly assigned into an SSI group or a control group. Three quarters (74 per cent) of the SSI group showed clinically meaningful reductions in the intensity and frequency of their symptoms, *regardless* of their original presenting problems. Eighteen months later, 60 per cent of those who benefited from the SSI maintained their early gains, even without receiving (or pursuing) any additional sessions.[109] The remaining 40 per cent appeared to maintain their gains as well, but they had opted to pursue one or two additional sessions in the interim.

Another series of trials, collectively including hundreds of adults and children, has shown that specific phobias (of flying, small spaces or spiders, among others) can be successfully treated via SSI. This particular SSI is based on 'exposure therapy', where clients are supported in facing their feared situation or object, step by step and in a gradual fashion, in order to acclimatise to facing their fear – while discovering that they can manage their distress more successfully than they expected.[110] When the two are compared head-to-head, exposure-based SSIs for phobias appear to be just as effective as multi-session alternatives.[86, 111] Other studies of exposure-based SSIs suggest they can have benefits for more than just phobias. Among adult survivors of the 1999 Turkish earthquake, an SSI led to meaningful declines in post-traumatic stress symptoms *two years later*, compared to a no-treatment control.[112] Similarly, in a small study of UK college students, an exposure-based SSI reduced symptoms of panic disorder three months later, compared to people who were placed on a waiting list for traditional therapy.[113]

Over the past six years, my research team and I have built and tested digital, self-guided SSIs for teens with depression and anxiety. Two of these SSIs – both twenty-to-thirty-minute, interactive activities completable from any internet-equipped device – have been tested in multiple clinical trials. (Both SSIs are also freely available online, if you would like to try them yourself – www.schleiderlab.org/YES – and adapted versions of these programmes are included as self-guided written activities on pages 160–187.) The first SSI, 'Project Personality', teaches that personal traits (like shyness, sadness or likeability) and mental health problems (like depression and anxiety) are *malleable* through a combination of personal effort and support (this is often called a 'growth mindset'). The second SSI, 'The Action Brings Change (ABC) Project', teaches how and why doing activities in line with your personal values – such as friendship, learning or generosity – can disrupt and reverse 'negative mood spirals' linked to depression.

In a 2019 *Atlantic* article on our team's digital single-session interventions, reporter Olga Khazan described her experience trying Project Personality herself, 'to see how teens might use it to essentially perform therapy on themselves, without the aid of a therapist':

> The strange little PowerPoint asks me to imagine being the new kid at school. I feel nervous and excluded, its instructions tell me. Kids pick on me. Sometimes I think I'll never make friends. Then the voice of a young, male narrator cuts in. 'By acting differently, you can actually build new connections between neurons in your brain,' the voice reassures me. 'People aren't stuck being shy, sad, or left out.' In the middle

> of my new-kid scenario, the program tells me the story of Phineas Gage, the 19th-century railroad worker whose behavior changed radically after a metal spike was driven through his skull . . . The program uses Gage's experience to suggest that personality resides at least partly in the brain. If a metal spike can change your disposition, Project Personality reasons, so can something less violent – such as a shift in your mind-set . . . Project Personality finds a way to make [this] uplifting: 'By learning new ways of thinking, each of us can grow into the type of person we want to be.'
>
> Toward the end, the activity asks me to reassure a friend who was snubbed by another friend in high school. What would I tell the friend about how people can change? It encourages me to apply what I just learned about personality and the brain. The total program takes me less than an hour to complete.[114]

The reporter summarised her understanding of the programme's main takeaway in a few simple statements: 'Your story isn't over till it's over. Your character's plot is still unfolding; there's still time to escape. Sometimes, it can take hours and hours on a therapist's couch to understand that. Maybe, just maybe, it could start to take less.'

In our first RCT of Project Personality with ninety-six high-symptom teens, the SSI increased teens' sense of control over their own emotions and actions. It also led to clinically meaningful reductions in teens' depression and anxiety symptoms *nine months later.*[115] For this RCT, it's worth noting that we created an 'active' comparison programme: a single-session online activity that encourages teens to share their emotions, without teaching specific skills (we call it the 'Sharing Feelings Project'). Comparing Project Personality to the Sharing Feelings Project helps us make sure that our SSI isn't just better than *nothing* – but that it's better than *something* that seems, on its face, like it might help.

Project Personality has also prevented increases in depression symptoms in a school-based RCT, which included 222 high-school girls in a low-income, rural US town.[116] And in an open trial (meaning that *everyone* got an SSI right away, with no control group), we saw that high-symptom teens who completed the ABC Project showed boosts in their perceived problem-solving abilities, along with feelings of agency and hope.[117]

And then the COVID-19 pandemic hit. School closures affecting more than 50 million students led to massive disruption of youth mental health supports. Given overwhelming needs, we decided to put our digital SSIs to the test: in a large, diverse teen sample, and in an incredibly high-stress context, could our digital SSIs *still* help alleviate depression symptoms? We secured grant funding from the National Institute of Health to find out. In our RCT of 2,452 teens (50 per cent youth of colour; 80 per cent sexual/gender minority youth; across all fifty US states), we saw that *both* of our SSIs outperformed the Sharing Feelings control. That is, they both led to meaningful three-month reductions in depression symptoms, hopelessness and restrictive eating in teens experiencing depression.[118] Project Personality also helped reduce anxiety and COVID-related trauma symptoms three months later. With these results, we finally felt confident in asserting that our digital SSIs really *could* help reduce teen depression symptoms – even amid unprecedented global stress.

Digital SSIs have also promoted mental health in contexts where treatment options are astoundingly scarce. For example, in a recent RCT including 103 high-school students in Kenya, Africa, a digital SSI called 'Shamiri-Digital' (*shamiri* means 'thrive' in Kiswahili) led to marked reductions in depression symptoms two weeks later, compared to a control programme teaching study skills.[119] Shamiri-Digital is a self-guided programme teaching users about growth mindset (similar to Project Personality), along with brief exercises designed to boost gratitude and help people identify their personal values. (A more recent and much larger trial, with 895 Kenyan students, found that two components of Shamiri-Digital – the 'growth mindset' and 'values' lessons – were the primary drivers of its positive effects on anxiety symptoms over time.)[120] Mental illness is not specifically mentioned in the programme, helping to make the SSI as non-stigmatising as possible. Kenyan youth are alarmingly unlikely to access mental healthcare, due to both the lack of trained providers[121] and social stigma in their communities (e.g. viewing mental health problems as weakness or evidence of having been bewitched by demons).[122] So, Shamiri-Digital (and especially its 'values' and 'growth mindset' lessons) may overcome context-specific barriers to accessing science-backed support.

Overall, there are many rigorous, randomised trials showing the potential of SSIs to reduce mental health problems. But you might be thinking – and you'd be right to! – that these are all *individual studies.* Couldn't they have been cherry-picked? What happens when you look at all of the SSI research put together, including *all* the work that's been done?

Systematic reviews are helpful safeguards here. These are specific types of reviews involving thorough, well-documented literature searches, which help researchers identify all existing studies on a topic. Some systematic reviews of treatment effects also include a 'meta-analysis' component, where researchers statistically combine results from all the studies they identify. This process allows them to estimate an overall, across-study treatment effect.

In line with individual SSI trials, several systematic reviews have supported the potential of SSIs for reducing anxiety, depression, trauma symptoms, behaviour problems and substance use, and have also indicated that SSIs can yield benefits that are *no different* from multi-session therapies, both for youths and adults.[72, 123, 124, 125, 126]

I was lucky to have the chance to lead one of them.

In 2016, as a clinical psychology graduate student, I grew more and more interested in how to maximise the odds that a client's first session – and often their *only* session, especially in lower-resource treatment settings – could truly, sustainably help them. As a youth-focused clinical psychology student, I launched a review project to learn whether single-session interventions could benefit children and teens *at all* – and, more generally, whether anyone had tried to find out. I had not heard of SSIs in my graduate training, so I was delighted to see that I was far from the first person to ask this question! Our resulting meta-analysis compiled results from fifty RCTs including 10,508 young people across Asia, North America, South America, Europe and Australia.[127] We saw that SSIs significantly reduced a wide range of youth mental health problems, compared to various controls, with only slightly smaller effects on symptom levels than multi-session (on average, sixteen-session) treatments.[128] SSIs' positive effects were *no different* for youth with more or less severe symptoms, or for youth with or without a formal diagnosis. In other words, SSIs seemed to benefit youths with mild, moderate and more severe mental health challenges. This meta-analysis also supported the promise of *online* SSIs: positive SSI effects emerged even for self-guided programmes (digital interventions that did not involve any therapist).

Another recent systematic review focused on SSIs for children and adults with anxiety disorders.[124] Here, the researchers focused exclusively on therapist-delivered SSIs for individuals with formal diagnoses. Across eighteen RCTs (four focused on children and fourteen focused on adults) including 1,090 people from Asia, North America, Europe and Australia, SSIs had highly consistent, positive effects on wide-ranging anxiety symptoms (panic attacks, social anxiety, phobias), along with common co-occurring problems (e.g. depression). SSIs outperformed no-treatment control conditions, and, yet again, showed benefits that did not differ from multi-session therapy alternatives.

So, yes. It appears that SSIs can 'work' in terms of improving mental health. But positive effects on mental health are not enough to warrant a large-scale roll-out of SSIs. In order to meet their theoretical promise to fill gaps in mental healthcare systems, SSIs must also be accessible, completable and experienced as helpful by those they aim to serve. Understanding SSIs' *acceptability* is just as important as establishing their benefits for mental health.

Can SSIs meet clients' needs?

SSI 'acceptability' can be measured in many ways, and all of them matter. Do people actually want SSIs when they are offered? Do they experience their SSIs as helpful in addressing their needs and concerns? Would they recommend SSIs to others? Fortunately, ample research speaks to these questions across a variety of settings, samples and SSI types.

Helpful acceptability data has emerged from existing SSI clinics and services (which remain few in number, but do in fact exist!). One especially rich study comes from a community mental health clinic in Victoria, Australia, which offers counselling services in a flexible manner; after completing their first session, clients are empowered to choose whether to schedule another one. Shane Weir and colleagues analysed service-use patterns of more than 115,000 clients who were seen at the clinic across three years.[54] They found that 42 per cent of these clients elected to have *just one session of treatment*, because they felt that their session had met their needs. In a separate study, ninety-eight clients at a Canadian clinic reported high satisfaction, lower distress and increased hope after an SSI, with 44 per cent reporting that the session was sufficient to meet their needs, and no further sessions were scheduled. In yet another study of treatment-seeking adults in Italy, forty-four out of eighty-five clients (52 per cent) considered their initial SSI to be sufficiently helpful, and they chose not to return for an additional session. Specifically, clients selected the following reasons for ending treatment after their SSI:

- 'I feel better, and I don't need more sessions' (nineteen clients, or 49 per cent)
- 'I need time to see how it goes' (eight clients, or 20 per cent)
- 'Practical issue unrelated to therapy' (four clients, or 10 per cent)
- 'I said no, but now I realise I do need more therapy' (three clients, or 8 per cent)
- 'The therapy or the therapist was not helpful' (one client, 2 per cent)[129]

A handful of other studies, albeit not on SSIs specifically, have explored clients' motivations for ending therapy within the first few sessions. For instance, in a study of treatment-seeking adults, between 14 and 46 per cent of clients who ended psychotherapy within the first few sessions did so because they felt sufficiently helped – even when SSIs were not explicitly offered.[130] In another study of 973 clients who began therapy at a Canadian counselling clinic and then stopped treatment early, close to half (43.4 per cent) cited 'feeling better' as their reason for ending treatment.[131]

Collectively, these results suggest – at least for some subset of clients – that an SSI might be sufficient to meet their needs and goals. And across studies and populations, the majority of people who end treatment after one session (or just a few) do so because their needs have been met.

But what about people who *do* want or need additional support, beyond an SSI? Are SSIs also acceptable and useful to them? Research from our lab suggests that they can be – and that SSIs may actually complement longer-term forms of care. Our team was especially interested in whether SSIs might be useful for people on waiting lists for outpatient psychotherapy. As discussed previously, waiting lists at mental health clinics are equal parts ubiquitous and damaging. They can range from weeks to months in length; people's symptoms tend to worsen while they're waiting; and longer waits predict poorer outcomes once treatment actually starts. In two trials (the first using a face-to-face therapy format, conducted pre-pandemic, and the second using a tele-therapy format, during the pandemic), we tested whether offering a solution-focused 'single-session consultation' to teens and adults while they were waiting for therapy might help reverse these trends. Everyone who took part in these trials had intentionally sought out multi-session, weekly mental health treatment (this is our Psychology Department clinic's main offering), so we were able to test whether SSIs might be acceptable and additively valuable for people already committed to longer-term care. Across both trials, among waiting-list clients who were offered the SSI, more than half opted to try it (51 per cent in the face-to-face trial; 65 per cent in the tele-therapy trial). Results were incredibly promising: regardless of delivery format (in-person versus telehealth), more than 90 per cent of clients rated the programme as being *mostly* or *very* helpful in addressing their concerns. Clients who completed the programme also reported reductions in hopelessness and increases in readiness for change from before to after the programme, along with declines in anxiety[132] and overall distress[133] two weeks later – *while they were still waiting for therapy to start.* Together, our results show that SSIs can serve as a highly acceptable – and clinically useful – form of support, even among people who are already pursuing other, more intensive treatment. We continue to offer our single-session consultation to all our waiting-list clients to this day (or, at least, as of my writing this sentence!).

And, finally – are digital, self-guided SSIs viewed as acceptable, too? These are the primary focus of our lab's research, and acceptability outcomes have been remarkably consistent. In all of our SSI trials, we use the same survey, called the 'programme feedback scale', to gauge the acceptability of our programmes.[134] This survey asks whether the SSI-user enjoyed the programme; whether they found it easy to understand; whether they found it easy to use; whether they tried their hardest on the programme; whether they found it helpful; whether they would recommend it to a friend; and whether they agree with the programme's message. Users rate each statement from one (really disagree) to five (really agree), with scores above 3.5 suggesting 'acceptability' in that domain. In online SSI trials involving more than 4,000 people – including parents experiencing anxiety,[103] adolescents with a history of self-injury,[104] youth experiencing depression,[118] and general teen and adult samples[117, 135] – six of our digital SSIs have been rated as uniformly 'acceptable', across *all* programme feedback scale domains, with most ratings above four out of five. As one teenage SSI-completer shared with us: 'This organised my thinking and different issues really well. And I felt very listened to, even though it was through a computer.'

All of these clinician-delivered and online SSIs share a critically important feature: *they are low-cost or free-of-charge to all who wish to access them*. Our lab's web-based SSIs are open-access for all to try, in multiple languages (so far, they're available in English, Spanish, Haitian Creole and Turkish). The clinics noted in Australia and Canada are free to clients, either because they are staffed by volunteers or thanks to government funding. In our Psychology Department clinic, SSIs are priced the same as a single session of standard therapy – a far lower access barrier than the cost of months or years of treatment. In other words, SSIs are highly unusual among forms of mental health support: when they are available at all, they are easily accessed at low or no cost to those in need.

SSIs work – they also just make sense

So far, SSIs appear to meet essential criteria for real-world dissemination: they can help reduce mental health problems, and they are acceptable to people they are designed to serve. Even beyond those critical elements, it seems well worth highlighting that – on so many levels, and considering the incredible need for services that are *available, affordable, empowering and non-stigmatising* – SSIs just make sense. As stated succinctly by Dr Michael Hoyt and colleagues:

> The most significant evidence supporting the adoption of a single-session therapy approach is client contact data that [we] all . . . need to address: *that a large number of clients will attend only one session, whether this is planned or not*. This simple finding has a profound implication for all approaches to counselling. Single-session therapy is a contextual model, a socially situated healing practice that endeavours to activate clients' own resources.[136]

In other words, SSIs are built for mental healthcare systems as they currently exist – not the mental healthcare systems we would prefer them to become. As noted in the previous chapter, there is ample evidence behind the statistic that 'one' is the most common number of psychotherapy sessions – including studies from hundreds of thousands of patients seeking mental health support from Australia,[54] America,[55] Canada,[59] Mexico,[60] Japan[61] and Spain.[62] Given this reality, our treatment systems cannot take for granted that people will return for session two.

The assumption that any therapeutic encounter might be the last – and committing to making the most of that single encounter anyway, because meaningful change in just one session is possible – is, to me, a powerful and humble way to meet clients wherever they are. This 'one-at-a-time' approach to SSI, where any session is treated as potentially the last, each encounter is optimised for clinical impact, *and* pursuing additional SSIs or other forms of support is always encouraged as needed, is patient-centred and empowering at its core.

Apart from acknowledging the realities of treatment-use patterns (and that, for some, a single-session intervention may be sufficient), SSIs may be accessed *at precise moments of perceived need.* At SSI walk-in counselling clinics – which have been up and running for decades, with more than forty walk-in SSI clinics in the Canadian province of Ontario alone,[137] and several in Australia[54] – people can access support when their motivation for change is greatest. Our lab's SSI for people on outpatient therapy waiting lists is offered to clients *at the moment when they initially seek treatment*, whereas their traditional, weekly therapy sessions begin weeks to months later. Likewise, our self-guided digital SSIs for adolescents and parents are freely available for use, whenever and wherever it suits those seeking support. There are no logistical hoops, no insurance-induced mazes, no multi-day intakes, no unacceptable delays. Clients can get help when it is best for them, rather than when it is best for the system.

Because SSIs can be delivered in multiple formats and settings, they empower clients to choose the type of support that fits them best. Those who prefer face-to-face therapy might stop by an SSI walk-in clinic. Others – whether due to stigma linked to service-seeking, a preference for self-help, or simple convenience – might instead opt to try an anonymous online SSI. Those interested in longer-term treatment might be offered an SSI while waiting for an available provider, in order to capitalise on natural motivation and prevent symptoms from worsening in the meantime. Adopting a 'one-at-a-time' approach to SSI services extends client empowerment further. Each SSI is optimised to help as much as possible, and further sessions are not assumed to be necessary; at the same time, SSIs are not capped, allowing clients to return for additional support as their needs evolve.

SSIs also make sense given their potential to reduce waiting times for treatment and boost the efficiency of care overall. At many outpatient therapy clinics (where the vast majority of speciality mental health services are presently offered), waiting-list management often becomes a full-time job for clinic staff. Dedicated 'intake coordinators' are often hired specifically to communicate with all waiting-list clients (sometimes managing *hundreds* at a given time) and address any emergent mental health crises or concerns. It is not uncommon for many waiting-list clients at these clinics to decline services once they are offered – either because they have since sought support elsewhere or because their motivation has waned across a multi-month wait – or for clients who *do* schedule an intake to never attend. At one Canadian clinic, shifting from by-appointment to walk-in, SSI/one-at-a-time services *eliminated the need for a waiting list altogether*, along with their need for an intake coordinator.[138] This approach may also carry positive ripple effects for ecosystems of treatment: after the proliferation of Canadian walk-in SSI clinics, mental health agencies have been able to drastically lessen staff members' time spent handling no-shows and cancellations,[138] allowing those same staff to establish and manage even *more* walk-in centres.[139]

Another example comes from one of the few walk-in SSI clinics in the United States, the Austin Child Guidance Center (ACGC) in Austin, Texas.[139] As described by Michael Slive and Monte Bobele, close to ten years ago, the ACGC had an unsustainably long waiting list for new clients. To remedy this challenge, they decided to launch a walk-in, SSI counselling service; the day it was launched, the ACGC discontinued their waiting list entirely. When new clients called to request an appointment, they were assigned to a long-term therapist if there was an appointment available within fourteen days; otherwise, the client could call back in a couple of weeks to check on appointment availability. But – regardless of long-term therapist openings – clients were informed of the walk-in SSI option, which could be used *as often as desired*, or until an appointment became available. Many who opted to walk in attended just one session, felt their needs had been met, and never made an appointment at all. Although ACGC's walk-in service is not 'free' for the clinic to provide – for instance, therapists must be available to see walk-in clients – they sustain consistent coverage through combinations of paid staff, trainee clinicians and volunteers, with staff who once managed the waiting list now overseeing the walk-in service or offering SSIs. ACGC has stuck with this model for close to ten years, serving more people for approximately the same cost.

Digital SSIs also hold promise as low-cost, high-impact mental health supports. For instance, the developers of Shamiri-Digital – the SSI mentioned earlier, which reduced depression symptoms in Kenyan youth – formally assessed the cost-effectiveness of their programme. They identified the primary 'costs' involved in SSI delivery as teachers' time (to oversee students who completed the digital SSI), plus internet and web-hosting.[140] Using these data points, the researchers found that it cost US $3.57 per student to offer Shamiri-Digital. Depending on the definition of 'clinically meaningful improvement', one student in every seven or ten completing Shamiri-Digital showed meaningful improvement in depression – translating to a cost of between US $25.35 and US $34.62. Any of these values, from $35 to $3, is a fraction of the cost of a single intake appointment with a private-pay psychotherapist – often more than $250 in major US cities – if you can schedule one at all.[141]

SSIs should not replace other services and mental health supports that are already available. But their clinical benefits, high acceptability and cost-effectiveness make them a common-sense mental health safety net: a layer of support accessible to all, helping fewer people fall through our systems' cracks than previously thought possible.

How exactly do SSIs help?

This is a complex question, and one that researchers haven't fully answered for *any* type of psychotherapy, let alone for newer delivery models like SSIs. Ultimately, the best answer will draw on multiple sources, from theory and research to lived experiences. The rest of this chapter will walk through some of the research pointing to some of the factors at play. Then, the next chapter will share perspectives from service users themselves, highlighting how they believe meaningful moments spurred lasting change on their roads to recovery.

In terms of what theory and research can teach us about how SSIs work, considering common factors across effective and acceptable SSIs, regardless of the specific SSIs' approaches, may be a useful starting point. Talmon has described specific factors – the single-session mindset and a context of competence – as potentially important.[142]

The single-session mindset

A single-session 'mindset' involves a set of guiding beliefs, present within the therapist or intervention and explicitly conveyed to the client. Any clinical encounter is understood as a singular event, because (1) something good can come from any one session, and (2) any one session could be the last. To establish this mindset within therapist-delivered SSIs, Hoyt and colleagues[82] suggest beginning sessions with some variant of the following (and indeed, we follow these guidelines in providing our SSIs for people on psychotherapy waiting lists):

> Many people who come here and talk about their problems find that just one time can help a lot . . . I'm willing to work hard today to help you get a better handle on things. Does that sound like something you'd like to do?

This framing establishes a shared expectation that *change, even in this very brief period of time, is absolutely possible.* Research on SSIs has taught us that this is entirely true, as have many studies showing that the vast majority of improvement in multi-session psychotherapy occurs within the first few sessions.[143] We also know that clients' expectations of change strongly shape their future engagement, motivation and symptom improvements during longer-term mental health treatment.[144] So, it makes perfect sense for SSIs to distil and capitalise on the power of believing that change is possible.

In our lab's digital SSIs, the message that 'change is possible in any given moment' is at the core of every intervention we build.

In addition to beginning our programmes by sharing that others have found this SSI to be helpful, we embed scientific explanations of *why* change is possible within the SSIs themselves. In one of our SSIs discussed earlier, Project Personality, we teach and discuss the concept of 'neuroplasticity' to explain why and how our emotions, symptoms, and coping skills can change – and that each action we take, no matter how small, can help bring that change to life. Likewise, in the ABC Project (another of our SSIs mentioned earlier), we explain that human brains can sometimes over-apply their naturally evolved 'must-avoid' response to potential threats – leading us to avoid *lots* of activities and situations, even those that once brought us joy. By intentionally practising activities that you find meaningful (such as spending time with friends, cooking for your family or playing with a puppy), you can recalibrate your brain's 'must-avoid' response and make more meaning each day. We emphasise, in both cases, that *all* human brains operate in these ways; all of us have some capacity for growth, and all of us can create meaningful moments, one step at a time. In addition to stressing the 'change is always possible' facet of the single-session mindset, we have found that incorporating brain science-rooted explanations both makes the SSIs' messages easier for teens to trust as universally true, despite the personal challenges they might have experienced, and also helps normalise the messages we aim to convey.

Our digital SSIs also include testimonials (personal narratives) from others who've experienced similar struggles, and meaningful changes, themselves. Stories are powerful communication tools, capturing hearts and minds to bring a given message to life. Systematic reviews have shown that testimonials greatly increase the persuasiveness of health-related messaging,[145, 146] including messaging around mental health.[147] For teenagers, the persuasive power of stories appears strongest when those stories come from their peers.[148, 149] So, our SSIs include stories from teens who've experienced depression (and positive change) themselves, in order to illustrate the programmes' core ideas. For instance, in this story (included in the ABC Project), 'Laura' shares how engaging in meaningful activities helped her through a particularly stressful time in her life:

> When I first started at my middle school, I felt really alienated. Most of the students at my school were white and valued different things than I did. As a Colombian American, many of my peers bullied and teased me for my culture and for caring about my academics. At the same time, I lost one of my closest friends to leukaemia. I found myself feeling overwhelmed; it was a really difficult time. Eventually, I tried to find ways to invest time in the things that I really valued most, starting with just reading part of a book I used to love. It was such a small thing, but it helped, and I felt like I could do more. I got involved with scientific research and chose to focus on dance as a creative outlet. I also made time to talk with my extended family over the phone and cook empanadas with my grandmother. Hearing my grandmother's stories about her childhood helped me to find support and strength in my culture. Talking with my sisters and mom helped me find social support when I needed it the most. Taking the time to do the things that really mattered to me, even a few minutes a day at first, helped me feel better over time.[150]

Consistently, teens who've tried either the ABC Project or Project Personality have shown decreases in hopelessness, increases in perceived control over their own emotions and behaviours, increased feelings of agency, and boosts in perceived problem-solving skills – suggesting that the SSIs *do* make change feel possible, at least a little more than before.[71, 115, 117] In one of our trials, teens who showed larger boosts in perceived control immediately after the SSI had the most substantial reductions in depression symptoms nine months later.[151] So, successfully instilling a 'single-session mindset' – that change is always possible, at any moment – seems to pay dividends later on.

Contexts of competence

A crucial assumption within SSIs, whether therapist- or self-guided, is that *all clients have inherent strengths and capabilities,* including the ability to alter their thoughts, feelings and actions to bring about positive change in their lives.[79] This might not sound like a radical idea in the context of mental health treatment. Unfortunately, clients often experience treatment as stigmatising, infantilising and undermining to their personal control[152] – especially teenagers, who often have little to no say in whether, when or where they access support. These trends in mental healthcare are echoes of a long-standing 'deficit focus' in psychiatry and clinical psychology, as Stefan Priebe and colleagues explain:

> The history of psychiatry has been dominated by a *deficit focus.* Treatments have been developed to remove or ameliorate the

> presumed deficit, even if assumptions on the specific nature of the deficits may often have been rather speculative. Such a deficit focus applies to models of pharmacological treatments as well as psychotherapeutic ones, such as psychoanalysis or cognitive behavioural therapy, that aim to solve an underlying conflict or to change maladaptive thinking and behaviours. This focus on deficits has a number of limitations; for example, it may strengthen a negative image of patients and reduce their sense of control, leaving them passive recipients of expert care.[153]

Rather than trying to 'fix' what clients *lack* and *cannot do,* SSIs – like many other recovery- and resource-orientated approaches to therapy – help clients harness their existing strengths in order to bring about change they wish to see. In this sense, the SSI therapist (or self-guided SSI programme) aims to foster a 'context of competence', where the client's sense of agency is bolstered, not diminished.

Empowerment is built into every aspect of SSIs, no matter their delivery format. Clients actively opt in to an SSI, whenever they perceive a need. Clients' knowledge, experiences and skills are centred as key to SSI effectiveness. And clients – not therapists – decide whether their SSI has fully met their needs, or whether further support might be helpful.

Establishing a 'context of competence' may be especially meaningful for youth-focused SSIs. Parents are de facto gatekeepers for their children's mental healthcare, and as a result, teenagers have breathtakingly little privacy or freedom to seek out support on their own terms. Our lab has led research on teens' perceived barriers to getting mental healthcare, and this short collection of quotes captures our general findings (these are free-text responses from teens aged thirteen to sixteen to an anonymous survey question: 'What got in the way of getting support for your mental health when you wanted it?').

- *'I couldn't tell my parents, they didn't understand.'*
- *'I was afraid to tell my parents.'*
- *'My parents' beliefs.'*
- *'. . . my parents don't take mental problems seriously . . .'*
- *'. . . I didn't want to ask my parents for permission, I don't want them to know I need help.'*
- *'I was scared to talk about it to my parents.'*
- *'I'm scared to ask my mother.'*
- *'Scared about talking about it with my parents.'*
- *'Parents don't believe in therapy.'*
- *'My parents don't believe I need help.'*

In our sample of 216 teens experiencing depression, 32 per cent of *all* the treatment-access barriers mentioned were directly linked to parents – either general family communication problems keeping teens from requesting parental permission to access care, or direct resistance from parents around mental health treatment more broadly.[154] So – because our SSIs have shown to be safe and helpful to teens who are struggling – they help maintain a 'context of competence' in part by allowing teens to opt in, anonymously and at any time, to our programmes, regardless of whether they can secure parental permission. Requiring parent approval for teens to try these online activities could prevent thousands of young people from receiving minimal-risk, free evidence-based support. To us, an 'opt-in' approach to digital SSIs for teens – and everyone, for that matter – is essential to prioritise in future roll-out plans.

We also focus on empowerment within the programmes themselves. In all of our SSIs, young people are treated as experts rather than passive recipients of support. For example, the opening portion of the ABC Project is presented to teens as follows:

> We need your help! We are scientists from Stony Brook University. We study the brain, emotions, and how teens cope with setbacks and stress. We work with kids and teens going through challenges in their lives, like dealing with worry, sadness, and stress. All teens experience these things at some point. So we are always trying to find new ways to help. Other teens have told us that they have found this short activity interesting and helpful. But we need your help explaining it in a better way to help more kids like you. Please help us and other teens like you by completing this activity carefully.[151]

And in fact, we actually *do* need their help. We incorporate teens' within-SSI responses into an open-access resource for others dealing with depression. At the end of the ABC Project, teens are invited to offer their 'best coping advice' to others experiencing mental health problems – and with their permission, their anonymous advice is shared on our lab's 'advice centre' (www.schleiderlab.org/advice) for others to read and learn from, hopefully helping them to feel less alone. So, in several respects, we treat teens as expert co-constructors of the SSIs we build – just as adult clients are 'co-constructors' of progress during therapist-guided SSIs.

Together, establishing a 'context of competence' and a single-session mindset can directly address clients' unmet needs for available, empowering, non-stigmatising and affordable mental healthcare.

Chapter conclusion

Unmet mental health needs are persistent and profound across the globe. Existing treatments were not built for broad accessibility, so it is critical to consider solutions that might fill its gaps. In this chapter, I've shared my take on why single-session interventions may offer a uniquely promising path toward accomplishing this goal – from how SSIs came to be, to the evidence that they work, to why they simply *make sense*, to reflecting on how they empower people to bring about meaningful change in their lives.

It bears repeating that SSIs cannot, and should never, replace other options and levels of support. And, at the same time, they *can* complement and extend existing support options in diverse, cost-effective, patient-centred ways. In order for SSIs to fill gaps in mental health ecosystems, the current systems must remain intact (and ideally, over time, must be improved from the top down). SSIs could serve as an additional, flexible, affordable means of offering clients in-the-moment, evidence-based help, in all the ways that existing options cannot.

We touched on *how* SSIs effect change, including the 'single-session mindset' (instilling the belief that meaningful change is always possible, even in a single session) and 'contexts of competence' (providing patient-centred, strengths-based, empowering forms of care). Virtually all effective SSIs seem to channel these two themes. But, as noted earlier, it is just as necessary (and unfortunately rare) to consider client perspectives and experiences on how, exactly, meaningful moments might spur impactful change. Their stories can enrich and hone our sense of how meaningful therapeutic moments come to be – and how, through future SSIs, we can help as many people as possible to create them.

3
Meaningful Moments in Action

You would think, given the dozens – to hundreds – of scientific studies on single-session mental health interventions, that client perspectives on turning points in recovery might be better represented by now. Or represented at all. Despite my best efforts (and I'm decently skilled at googling), I came up empty when searching for a collated, organised set of personal stories about 'meaningful moments' or 'turning points' in mental health recovery journeys. This strikes me as a critical gap in our understanding of exactly *how* brief interventions, or meaningful moments, can lead to lasting change – and how we might help others learn to create meaningful moments, too – both in and beyond SSIs. That gap is one of the primary reasons I decided to write this book.

SSI as a treatment delivery model is client-centred at its core. But research on SSIs has rarely centred clients' experiences of recovery. This omission is not specific to SSI research, by any means. Most research on psychotherapy has prioritised quantitative data points over personal narratives and experiences. Of course – as a primarily quantitative researcher – I believe empirical data is crucial. But it is not everything. Scores on depression-rating scales and multi-level statistical models cannot shed light on how clients actually *understand* moments that made a lasting impact on their recovery – the sort of moments that SSIs are thought to spark, which can catalyse lasting positive change. These meaningful moments (or turning points, or corrective experiences – there are lots of ways to describe them) are embodied encounters that no one-to-five rating scale can capture. But speaking from experience, I know that they are real. Thinking back across my cycles through anorexia treatment, I still carry a few key moments with me. In my mind, I can easily summon up the brief interactions that helped me, finally, to see myself and my future in a different light. Those moments surprised me, challenged me and helped me – as one man I interviewed beautifully phrased it – to 'do the next right thing.'

I believe that listening to real people's experiences of recovery turning points could strengthen the power and focus of single-session interventions. Perhaps, by capturing common themes that unite people's turning points, we can learn more about how and why SSIs seem to spark real change. Perhaps these stories can add a dimension and depth that RCTs and population-wide surveys cannot.

This part of the book integrates personal interviews and written survey responses from ninety-eight remarkably generous human beings from all over the world. All of them have sought out mental health treatment at some point in their lives, many while facing immense personal and structural obstacles. And all of them saw my Twitter post asking for volunteers to share their own 'turning points' in recovery from mental illness. They read my definition – 'specific, brief moments that made a lasting impact on your journey toward mental health' – and knew precisely what I meant, because they had experienced it too. This part of the book is a reflection, celebration and attempted synthesis of what we can learn about 'turning points' based on their lived experiences – and how we can use this knowledge, in and beyond single-session interventions, to help others turn toward change, too.

There are several things this chapter of the book is not. It is not a nationally representative sampling of therapy experiences, nor is it a comprehensive list of the many, likely infinitely varying ways that 'turning points' can show up in someone's life or recovery. It is not the universal truth. It is not an instruction manual. It is not a peer-reviewed scientific paper. It is not a series of interviews with people who've been through SSIs, because most people (despite the studies discussed in Chapter 2) still do not know what those are.

It is a collection of rich, personal stories, from volunteers who generously agreed to contribute to this book, which may humanise the thousands of data points suggesting that brief experiences can lead to lasting change. It is an opportunity to learn what 'decreases in hope' and 'increases in agency' actually look like, in the context of someone's recovery. It is an exploration of how it feels, in the moment, to undergo a 'corrective emotional experience', whether it occurs in or out of therapy. It is a testament to the diversity of where, how and why meaningful moments can occur. And it may help us learn, or at least begin to learn, how to harness single-session interventions to *make* more of those moments, both for ourselves and for others who are struggling.

First, for context, I'd like to share a bird's-eye view of the volunteers who shared their stories. Here is the text from the request they all replied to, which I posted on social media during the summer of 2021:

> My name is Jessica Schleider. I'm a psychology professor and founder and director of the Lab for Scalable Mental Health. I study ways to improve access to mental healthcare using brief, barrier-free interventions. Based on this and related work, I'm writing a non-fiction book, and as part of this project, I am seeking volunteers to share their stories about lived experience with mental health challenges. I'm seeking stories about 'turning points' in people's journeys toward recovering from, or living with, mental health challenges. By 'turning points', I mean specific moments or experiences that made a clear difference in your own recovery or coping. Turning points can happen anywhere, in or out of formal treatment. I've had turning points in my own mental illness recovery – and I suspect that others have, too. If you are open to sharing your story for possible inclusion in my book, I would be grateful for your response to this five-minute, ten-question survey.
>
> Anybody in any location is welcome to share their story. The survey asks for your email address, so I can follow up with any clarifying questions and let you know whether your story will be included in the book. Otherwise, you can

> skip any questions you'd rather not answer, and you may stop the survey at any time. Your answers will not be used or shared for any reason outside of the book. If your story is included, I will use pseudonyms and change identifying details to protect your privacy.

The survey asked volunteers to share the following: basic demographic information (age, country of origin, race/ethnicity, gender identity); the types of mental health problems they have experienced, in their own words; whether or not they had experienced difficulty accessing mental health treatment (and, if so, what barriers they faced); and finally, any recovery 'turning points', with the following open-ended question:

> Some people experience 'turning points' when coping with or recovering from mental health challenges. By 'turning points', I mean specific moments, realisations, conversations or experiences that made a clear difference in your own recovery or coping. Turning points can happen anywhere, in or outside of formal treatment. Please share as much or as little as you would like about 'turning points' in your own mental health coping or recovery journey.

Ninety-eight people completed the survey in full, and (with their permission) I followed up with fifteen of them for face-to-face interviews to learn more about their experiences. I've attempted to weave together their stories and perspectives, from both written and interview-based responses, below.

The volunteers (who were the same group described on page 49) had experienced a wide array of mental health challenges, with most reporting multiple problems as opposed to just one:

Percentage of volunteer survey respondents (out of 98) self-identifying with a past or current history of different mental health problems. Most volunteers listed more than one type of problem.	
Anxiety	55% (54 respondents)
Depression	67% (65 respondents)
Psychosis	6% (6 respondents)
Bipolar disorder	4% (4 respondents)
Attention-deficit hyperactivity disorder	4% (4 respondents)
Suicidal thoughts or behaviours	33% (32 respondents)
Borderline personality disorder	8% (8 respondents)
Eating disorder	10% (10 respondents)
Substance/alcohol use disorder	12% (12 respondents)
Obsessive compulsive disorder	20% (20 respondents)
Non-suicidal self-injury	16% (16 respondents)

Their responses to the 'turning points' question spanned an incredible range of settings and circumstances. For some, turning points occurred within formal treatment. But for many, they unfolded in other contexts entirely: during a university lecture; through exchanges with friends, partners or strangers; at home, alone; while sitting by an especially beautiful lake; in finding community; after gaining acceptance to a graduate programme or receiving a job offer; after moving across the country; while watching a YouTube video. All of the stories are entirely unique, as all coping and recovery journeys are bound to be. And, at the same time, themes and trends emerged that seem to warrant reflection.

The clearest connector across virtually *all* the turning points was the experience of realising hope that change might be possible, where little such hope had existed before. In fact, the word 'hope' was used by nearly a third of volunteers in their written descriptions of turning points, and was also used by most of the people I had the opportunity to interview. But 'increases in hope', on its own, did not seem like the most useful focus for this part of the book. We already know from the science discussed in Chapter 2 that feelings of hope tend to increase after SSIs, whether they are therapist-delivered or self-guided. What struck me most were people's descriptions of *how* that hope was generated – the types of experiences, encounters and realisations that suddenly made 'hope' feel a little bit more real.

In reviewing all ninety-eight responses, I tried my best to

create a coding system to capture common themes.* To unpack my process: while reading through each response, I generated a list of phrases and concepts that seemed to summarise some aspect of the 'turning points' each person described. This led me to an initial list of sixteen possible themes.

Next, I coded whether each of these sixteen themes seemed to be 'present' or 'absent' from each person's description of their turning points. Finally, I tallied up the results to identify the most common themes.

Five of the sixteen themes emerged in more than 15 per cent of written responses, with the other themes appearing in one to eight responses each. Importantly, these five themes seemed relevant to nearly everyone in the sample: ninety-two out of ninety-eight responses described a turning point that fitted *at least one* of these five themes.

So, these are the themes, or *pathways to hope*, that I will focus on from here. The pathways that came up most frequently were:

1. *Surprising yourself* (present in 21 per cent of turning-point descriptions). Doing something, even something small, you were once certain you could not.

* I should mention a caveat. This approach to identifying themes across many written responses is often called 'thematic analysis'. In formal research studies, best practices for thematic analysis involve *multiple* coders, who independently review text and generate possible themes. This step allows the coders to reach agreement on themes they have each individually identified. To protect the privacy of the volunteers who contributed their stories to this book, I did not involve anyone else in my efforts to code these responses. As conveyed to the volunteers, this survey was not a formal research study, but rather a means of gathering information for this book. I share the percentages across my own identified themes to make my thought process as clear as possible to readers.

2. *Feeling seen* (present in 53 per cent of turning-point descriptions). Experiencing newfound validation from others. Feeling genuinely and fully understood.
3. *Seeing others* (present in 16 per cent of turning-point descriptions). Discovering that other people are going through or have overcome struggles similar to yours. Feeling less alone and more supported.
4. *Reclaiming your narrative* (present in 47 per cent of turning-point descriptions). Realising the future you want for yourself, and taking a first step toward making that future possible.
5. *Giving back* (present in 16 per cent of turning-point descriptions). Feeling empowered through supporting others through struggles similar to your own.

Of course, these categories are not mutually exclusive. Many people's descriptions seemed to span two or three of them, particularly for people who described more than one turning point in their lives. Each pathway toward hope materialised in different ways for different people. So their words, not mine, are by far the best means of showing you what I mean.

Pathway one: Surprising yourself

Several volunteers shared moments in which they observed themselves doing something they never imagined they could do.

In some cases, this involved trying a skill taught in therapy for the first time; in others, it involved entering a new environment and coping more successfully than they'd imagined they could. Three examples come from JM, CL and RC – who each vividly recall discovering coping capabilities they never knew they had.

JM, aged twenty-seven (USA)

JM had struggled with overwhelming emotions since childhood, and in middle school, they discovered self-harm as a means of managing them. As a teenager, they felt discouraged from seeking support; their mother 'just didn't believe in mental illness . . . she hoped that I would just be able to stop'. It was not until college that they sought out therapy for the first time – when their insurance finally covered sessions, and they could seek out support on their own. '[The therapist] just immediately recognised that there was a big issue with emotion regulation, impulsive self-destructive behaviour, so she immediately jumped into teaching me dialectical behavioural therapy (DBT) skills.' But *learning* the skills, they said, was not enough to facilitate change. In fact, JM explained:

> I was like, maybe [those skills] work for other people, but not me. The skills just won't apply to me. For me there's no control. So, [my therapist] gave me the worksheets and she said, 'Just record your thoughts, feelings and actions the next time one of these spirals happens.' And for the first couple of weeks, I just didn't want to do it. I didn't try. But I really do remember very clearly the first time I actually felt like I had

> the ability to pause, notice what was happening, and actually choose to do something self-destructive or not. And it was wild. I got really upset about something pretty small, and I was feeling the impulse to react in any number of harmful ways . . . and I just, I noticed how I was feeling.

JM was shocked. The skills weren't supposed to work for them. Yet somehow, after trying them out just once, they actually did.

JM continued:

> It did feel dramatic. It felt notable . . . I was in an enormous amount of pain, but I just didn't know what to do, so I was wasting my energy, and not really expecting anything I could do to help me in any way . . . Clearly, I was missing something. I was trying very hard, but it wasn't working. And eventually, when I tried [the skill], it really, really made a lot of sense. It really seemed like this was the thing that would work for me.

This was JM's crystal-clear turning point: experiencing total surprise that, for the first time, they had managed to help themselves feel markedly better, through something they did themselves, in a way they had assumed was impossible.

Change didn't happen right away for JM. At first, they were mainly confused by their turning point, and how well they had managed to help themselves. (They didn't even mention the experience to their therapist!) It took time, practice and patience for their self-harm urges to gradually improve. What *did* seem to make a lasting difference, from that brief moment, was their surprising realisation that they might actually have the capacity to help themselves in the long term: the sudden sense of possibility that a different future might be within reach.

> Once I got attuned to noticing what made a difference – and also what I stood to gain – that mattered a lot. For a while, I wasn't sure what it would even be like to *not* feel terrible all the time. I remember at one point feeling like, maybe I was just an apple that had rotted all the way through and there was no apple left. I wasn't sure, if I cleared out all the rot, if there would even be any apple left. I wasn't sure if there would be a person there. That's something I remember thinking . . . it seems like there's still a person in here who is capable of feeling good . . . And it's worth putting in the effort to be able to feel that way more of the time.

They went on to describe the mindset shift their turning point (which they call their 'change moment') created for them, which they believe made their future improvements possible:

> It's always a little bumpy, but I think of things as having been mostly uphill from that change moment . . . The practice of trying to master these skills, the idea that it wasn't going to all be better right away, that helped me stay motivated. I was in a very all-or-nothing mindset before my change moment. Any setback made me think I'd lost all progress I had made. But I think with this skills mindset, when there were times when things got a little bit worse or got harder to maintain,

> *I knew I could do something*. And I did what I could, and it never spiralled all the way back to where I had been before. It felt like a mindset that I gained that changed things after that.

CL, aged twenty-four (UK)

We first met CL in Chapter 1. After attempting to seek depression treatment through primary care, and later through her college's counselling centre, she was met with months- to years-long waiting lists at every turn. Eighteen months after she first attempted to access treatment, CL made an attempt to end her life. 'It's unfortunate that it had to get to a crisis point for me to receive any sort of care . . . But that was the only way to get to the top of the waiting list.'

CL's turning point came nine months after her attempt. By then, she had transitioned out of crisis care, finding herself truly 'on her own' for the first time since her crisis point. Shortly after, the COVID-related lockdowns were announced, and she feared what isolation might mean for her mental health:

> I had come out of crisis support, and I was referred to therapy – back to a waiting list. This was right when they announced the lockdown . . . I moved into an apartment on my own . . . I had to face my fears of being alone during that time. And I still remember, having that moment of sitting in my bedroom and looking around, and realising that I was actually on my own, just doing activities. I didn't *need* other people, or my phone, or to ring people in order to feel okay.

She watched herself, amazed at her ability to feel okay, to simply *be.* At the time, she felt acutely aware of her realisation that she could feel good, and safe, all on her own – and she found it deeply motivating:

> I was very much aware of it. I became aware of it in the moment. I realised that, actually, this is happening for me now. This is really, really good. It threw me into this momentum of seeking that feeling – wanting to feel good alone.

And she was able to keep that momentum going, even a year later:

> It was obviously difficult, but now, over a year since then, I literally love being alone! Like, I love it *again* – which I did when I was a teenager, but I'd lost it. It really feels good to look back on that moment, and have it in my brain, so when I'm struggling, I can be, like – no, it's okay, I've done this.

Similarly to JM, CL emphasised that her turning point, on its own, was far from a cure. Rather, it revealed a new path forward that she'd never realised was there.

> Life is still a rollercoaster. Even though I've had those moments, it doesn't mean my mental illness has gone away. But those moments have helped me continue living. Without them, I don't know that I could have kept going. They helped me realise what I'm capable of.

RC, aged twenty-three (USA)

RC shared two distinct turning points on their journey toward managing obsessive compulsive disorder. The first one occurred in their teenage years, before they had a label for their diagnosis – or even understood their experiences as something warranting support: 'I didn't think there was anything I really needed help for. I just thought it was something that kind of everyone dealt with, like having an overactive imagination.' Their first turning point – when they were able to act in opposition to their compulsions for the first time – came at a time of incredible personal challenge. When their mother became ill, RC's 'active imagination' (a compulsion to lock their bedroom door overnight) starkly conflicted with their drive to care for their mother:

> My mom was sick. And she slept in the other half of the house at night . . . I could hear her if she yelled, even with the doors closed, but I also had this fear that she would slip away in the night, and I wouldn't be able to hear her or do anything about it . . . So I slept with my door open. It was kind of like a self-made exposure therapy: every night I forced myself to [lie in bed with] my back to the door, [facing] my wall with [the door] open, and let the sounds of my mom's TV from across the house put me to sleep . . . It was really, really hard. But the fear of her needing me in the middle of the night and me not being able to hear because my door was closed completely overrode any of the fears I had.

So, with overwhelming difficulty, RC persisted. For the first time, they were determined to stop acting on their compulsion. And it was *hard*. There were moments when 'it was so, so lonely . . . I just had to cope with crawling out of my skin, just not sleeping'. But they also remember the moment when they paused, and reflected, and everything changed:

> It was after I got through the first week. That was it. I was like, that's got to be the hardest part. We got it on lock. Now let's just keep going.

After that first exhausting week, reflecting on their own strength – and allowing themselves to *own* that strength – was precisely what RC needed to continue what mattered to them most: being there for their mother through her illness. And they realised, from that point on, that their thoughts were just that: thoughts. Not requirements. Perhaps their 'active imagination' wasn't in control, after all.

Although it felt significant, this turning point was not a panacea. RC continued to experience other compulsions and obsessions, which they still didn't fully understand. It was not until RC began college, and enrolled in a clinical psychology class, that they finally gained the vocabulary to describe their lifelong challenges – and a second turning point helped them heal for the long term.

Pathway two: Feeling seen

RC, aged twenty-three (USA), continued

RC's story continues with a second turning point, through another pathway entirely, a few years after their first. The power of feeling seen, validated and understood is something that most of us have experienced at one time or another. Being known, both to yourself and to people you care for, brings safety. It fosters peace, closeness and comfort. For RC, it brought self-understanding they had never experienced – right in the middle of class:

> It was my sophomore year of college. I was sitting in a lecture about anxiety disorders. The professor was going through the symptoms and I was like, *Holy shit*! I had that moment. I was like, okay. Wow. I had to process it in class. Things all kind of came together. He was talking about the magical thinking, and I was like, *I remember that*! I didn't know it was something you could get help for. I didn't grow up with internet access, so it wasn't like I could google, 'What's wrong with me?' and talk with other people who'd [had] similar experiences. It was just me and my mom and our little country home. My town is very traditionally conservative . . . that's very much the dominant culture.

That single lecture gave RC the validation they needed to feel that change, through treatment, might be possible – something they had never once considered might be true. They continued:

> I really liked that I had something to name it. It was very validating and freeing. It wasn't a flaw of my personality and beyond my control, or an overactive imagination . . . like, that's just not me reading too many fantasy books as a kid. This was something that other people who are rational and know themselves and are introspective have experienced, too. I knew something was wrong at the time, but I couldn't unlock it. It wasn't a deficiency – it was something else, and that something made sense. I just remember coming out of that class. I got a coffee afterwards, exhausted, but in a good way. It felt like a whole new page.

With renewed self-understanding, and a sense of amazement at the power of simply *feeling understood*, RC began to open up to others about their experiences, talking to both friends and their therapist. It motivated them to make a concrete plan for OCD relapse prevention. It sparked a newfound confidence in coping that made them excited and proud.

> I wasn't very open about my experiences before I had the language of OCD. After that, I had no issues talking about mental health. Having [the language of OCD] and being able to talk about it . . . was really, really, really amazing. And that wasn't even what I was really seeking therapy for in college – but I was able to say, this is in my history, and it might come up again, like during transitions, like living somewhere new. But I finally knew what to do. I knew how to talk about it. I could make a plan – this is how we're going to combat this if it comes up.

Yet again, we see turning points serving as catalysts for upward spirals. The ripple effects of positive emotions, effective coping and open communication can compound and expand over time to bring about change that matters.

Before our interview ended, I asked RC for their take on how 'turning points' fit into years-long journeys toward recovery. They believe the two are very much compatible: that is, people may progress through coping and recovery over long periods of time, while also experiencing specific, small experiences with outsized impact:

> For some people, I think recovery is a very slow and gradual process where like, yeah, it is every day and everything you do, and you might have just eased into it almost like a hobby, building a skill. But like, I think most people would resonate with the [idea that] there's a turning point in this. For sure, I know I did. It was very easy to identify right off the bat; like, that's when things changed. Maybe there were a couple points that kind of helped reinforce the turning point, but there was a definite time when the [improvement] curve was flat – and then it suddenly started going up, and I knew it could keep going.

NL, aged twenty-eight (Malaysia)

Mental illness stigma persists across the globe, albeit in different forms. When NL began experiencing symptoms of depression, her family assumed a spiritual cause, leaving NL with an overwhelming sense of shame when her 'healing sessions' failed to help:

> Unfortunately, our culture tends to believe in spiritual healing. I was forced to undergo a few spiritual healing 'sessions'. The ritual in itself was pretty harmless; just some prayers and random gestures from the healer. But I remembered feeling like a failure, like God was punishing me, because they told me that my depression was due to my lack of faith.

With little understanding of what NL was experiencing, her family reacted in ways that left her wondering if her depression really *was* her own fault:

> My family members also tended to guilt-trip me. I wasn't capable of going to school while I was depressed. I had family members telling me I was being disobedient to my parents, that I should feel sorry for making them worry. In one such encounter, it exacerbated – and almost made me go through with – my suicidal thoughts. I was also described as a 'problematic child' by an employee of a private education centre.

Feeling unseen can be unimaginably lonely. Without support from those she loved the most, and with little knowledge about the nature of clinical depression, NL was left to assume that she *was* to blame for her symptoms, as well as her family's concern.

She never received the necessary tools to even see *herself.* Even when she first received a formal diagnosis, she assumed it didn't apply to her: 'Due to the pervasive stigma [around] mental illness, I was ashamed and in denial when I first received my diagnosis.'

And then, a chance encounter with an online article shifted NL's perspective entirely:

> It wasn't until I read an online article about depression, which was quite descriptive about the symptoms, that I began to accept I had depression. I felt 'seen', as if the article was written about me. After that moment, I read up about how to manage depression. I found exercise to be one of the ways to help cope. I began enjoying exercise at home. I also found reading, writing and drawing [helped] me process what I experienced.

On its own, feeling 'seen' by the article did not cure NL's depression. But it *did* unlock the possibility of taking steps to heal, by allowing her to feel understood – and to understand herself – in a way she never had before.

HK, aged twenty-five (USA)

Like NL and RC, HK shared feelings of shame, guilt and confusion about her social anxiety, which she harboured (and hid) from an early age:

> When I was a child, I couldn't speak in school. I remember feeling extremely confused [and] humiliated, as if it was my

> fault for not trying hard enough to be like all of the other children around me. I made constant efforts from the time I was a young child to hide my confusion and hurt from all of the adults in my life as I braved many stressful experiences throughout the early years of my education. I knew it was not normal to be the way that I was, and I didn't want to draw attention to what seemed to be shortcomings [for which] I was at fault. Essentially, I didn't get the treatment I needed because there was a lack of awareness surrounding selective mutism in the early 2000s. This resulted in a deep-rooted sense of shame that I carried with me up until very recently.

Also like NL and RC, HK described a transformative moment of feeling 'seen' through simple, brief education during a high-school psychology class:

> The first big turning point in my life was when I took a psychology class in high school and learned for the first time about common mental health disorders, such as anxiety and depression. I [had never been] taught about mental health in school, and I didn't even know that other people in the world struggled with internalising psychopathology, just as I always had. I think for the first time, I felt a sense of validation, and [this] newfound awareness enabled me to finally begin making sense of my own story. Not only did I realise I needed to get myself help, but for the first time in my life, I felt like I [had] found something that was worth working for. I made a decision to pursue psychology in order

> to educate myself and others about mental illness, raise awareness of early risk factors, and ultimately work toward preventing other children from experiencing what I once went through.

HK reported a second turning point several years later, when she felt particularly seen during a psychotherapy session. This second meaningful moment provided powerful affirmation of her first.

> During one meeting, my therapist said a few very simple sentences that inadvertently encouraged me to begin a new journey of healing, acceptance and self-love: 'You're too hard on yourself. It's common for people with social anxiety to lack life experiences.' I immediately thought back to when I first realised that other people in the world suffer from anxiety in my high-school psychology class. It was the validation.

HK left her session feeling not only understood by her therapist, but empowered to more fully understand herself. She felt liberated to embrace compassion (instead of blame) toward her past and present self, along with newfound hope for her future:

> I was once again reminded that there is a very real thing out there known as anxiety, and I, like many others, have come to know its devastating effects. I did not choose the way that my story began, nor did I choose to suffer the long-term consequences of growing up with an undiagnosed and untreated anxiety disorder. However, I did choose to try my

> best at every stage in my life despite my circumstances. That may not sound like enough for everyone I will meet, but it is enough for me to be at peace with myself and work toward the changes that I would like to see in the world with confidence.

RA, aged twenty-seven (USA)

RA's story follows a remarkably similar pattern to those of HK, NL and RC; from a young age, she felt that something, somehow, was different about her. And at times, that difference felt scary, burdensome and near-impossible to sustain.

> I feel like I came out of the womb as an anxious child. I have visions of myself crying over my homework in kindergarten. I don't even know when I knew that help was a thing that I could get, that was out there. But I think I knew at least from [my] late childhood [or] early teen years, that something wasn't right, and I couldn't see the rest of my life continuing, feeling the way that I felt.

RA's self-stigma – or, in her words, the 'seed of wondering if there's something fundamentally wrong with me' – grew more complex when she decided to pursue a mental health career:

> You know, I'm in the [mental healthcare] field. I want to be in this field for a long time. Up until very recently, I have harboured this huge fear of being 'found out' – of having people that I respect and look up to finally knowing that I, a person with lived experience of mental illness, have

> infiltrated this field. But also that I am this person who struggles. And also what that would mean for questioning my clinical judgement, my research, my skill – all of those things . . . I really care about being seen as super competent.

As a brief aside: RA is far from unusual, and also, her concerns make perfect sense. Within the clinical psychology profession, openly discussing your lived mental illness experience remains taboo, and disclosure can lead to unwanted career consequences and opportunity loss.[155, 156] But paradoxically, in a recent study of nearly 1,700 clinical psychologists and trainees across the US and Canada, over 80 per cent reported experiencing mental health problems at some point in their lives, and nearly half (48 per cent) self-disclosed a diagnosed mental health disorder.[155] Lived experience among clinical psychologists is the rule, not the exception – but stigma against mental illness remains deeply ingrained, even among those who dedicate their careers to treating it.

With this context, it makes sense that RA's turning point came through an exchange with another professional mental healthcare provider: her therapist. And it made precisely the difference she needed.

> A huge turning point occurred when my current therapist told me that my prior experiences could be an asset to my clients and to my research, rather than a thing that I needed to feel ashamed [of]. Having her tell me that my experiences could not only not hold me back, but . . . could actually [enhance]

> my ability to benefit and validate and understand my clients, and to [ask] questions that people without my experiences wouldn't think to ask. Also, knowing that I didn't necessarily have to be light years ahead of my clients in terms of my own progress in my recovery – knowing that it's okay to be here, walking with them . . . that has value. My 'stuff' doesn't have to be in a box, on a shelf, in order to inform how I help others in a meaningful way. I think learning that was also really helpful.

This moment helped RA start to break through the shame that had followed her for years:

> Shame was this huge cloud over everything. Lessening that shame not only allowed me to bring my experiences in[to] my work more, but it also helped me reach out for help, and be more open about my experiences overall.

Turning points are where change begins, not where change ends.

Pathway three: Seeing others

MW, aged sixty-six (USA)

All of us are social beings at our core. Humans are evolutionarily driven to avoid and combat loneliness – and, in fact, your brain and body registers threats of loneliness similarly to threats of physical violence. So, it may be unsurprising that turning points can involve moments of feeling less alone, and the profound internal shifts that often follow.

Upon his first admission to a locked psychiatric hospital for substance use and addiction, MW described precisely this kind of experience. He entered the hospital with a seemingly locked-in feeling of hopelessness: 'I kind of had this idea that maybe I [could] just live on the back ward of some hospital forever,' he shared. But that feeling's foundations started to shift at a meeting he attended on his first night there.

> The first night I was in that locked psychiatric ward, there was the first kind of [group therapy meeting]. And there was a guy in that meeting. And he was one of those kinds of guys, it looks like his face has lived in different places. Tattoos of railroad tracks over his arms. And he was telling this story in this meeting, and I mean, it was familiar. I'm thinking that the reasoning was familiar to me, about a career change from armed robbery to strong-arm robbery, because you might go out of strong-arm robbery and just say, 'It was a fight' – and then even if you did get convicted, the charges would be lower . . . I really identified with that way of parsing how to live life.

But what surprised MW was not that this man had endured difficulties similar to his own. It was the path he had forged since enduring them.

> But he wasn't living that way anymore. He was actually a tech working at the psych ward. And I remember him saying, 'You know, you don't have to live that way.' I did not

> know that. I mean, I really, really did not know that. And I had a sense that . . . he knew what he was talking about. Like, he wasn't just bullshitting. He had lived where I had lived. But he wasn't living there anymore, you know. I was in a locked ward, and he had keys, and I didn't. And that wasn't a mistake.

After that first meeting, MW and the psych tech spent more time together. Slowly, his belief solidified that a different future might actually be possible.

> I remember him . . . he took me to meetings and coffee, and the whole time I'm waiting for the other shoe to drop, like, what assets could I possibly have? But it never did. I don't think I really recognised what he was doing until after I lost track of him. Before that, I just had no idea my life could be different than it was. Except maybe that it would just keep getting worse, and that [the] people [closest to] me would take more damage . . . So, seeing [him] was something of a revelation. But you know, people who have not been in the midst of such things . . . [they would say], 'Of course.' But it wasn't clear to me.

DM, aged thirty-two (Spain)

Midway through DM's college career, her thoughts began to frighten her. This experience was not altogether new; she had a history of mood problems, and her mother had encouraged her to seek treatment before. But now her distress felt urgent and unfamiliar. She worried about keeping herself safe. Within a few hours of sharing these worries with her residence director, DM found herself admitted to a psychiatric inpatient unit for the very first time.

At first, the pre-existing stigma she felt around mental illness left her hesitant to interact with other patients: 'I was kind of scared, because I didn't understand mental illness. I thought of the scary tales they tell you when you're little – that they kill, that they're insane, they're crazy.' But following some early interactions, DM's understanding of them – and in turn, of herself – began to shift dramatically.

> I started to have breakfast and did a group therapy session with them. We painted how we were feeling, I think. And I started to realise they were people like me. I was closer to them than to the rest of the world. We shared some great suffering. Each person was different, but there were fathers. There were people like me. Students from the universities. People had depression, bulimia, schizophrenia, but we all shared something. We were isolated from the world, because the world had isolated all of us. I felt more understood by them than by the doctors and the nurses. They were great professionals. But I realised that, yes, we were the patients, but it was like our voices were not valuable. At that point, I found myself giving this motivational speech to the other patients. I told them that they really inspired me. They were strong. They were fighting to have a normal life, a normal

> marriage, or live the life they wanted. They were fighting to be a part of this world. I just wanted to say to them that they were the biggest part of my recovery.

DM's turning point – realising the humanity of, and her deep connection with, other patients on her unit – quickly became a powerful motivator on her journey toward recovery. She felt empowered by her new community to heal through shared struggle, stress and support:

> They were just like me. We were normal people. We needed help, but we were not insane. Also, it created a community. I never had that before. If you think of the LGBTQ community, for example, they needed a community, a collective, to see one another, in order to feel understood. That's what these patients were for me. When they were sad, I felt sad. There was such a connection between them and me.

Pathway four: Reclaiming your narrative

DM, aged thirty-two (Spain), continued

In addition to meeting and connecting with patients in her psychiatric unit, DM described another key turning point. This one occurred just before she was admitted to the hospital. In this moment, she found herself empowered, for the first time, to intentionally step toward a future she genuinely wanted. A future starkly different from the one that often felt inevitable.

> At that time, I was living in a student residence. I had given my pills to the head mistress of the residence, because I didn't trust myself. I didn't have any pills – so I looked for other ways. I was really planning. But I started to have opposite feelings then. I wrote the director a message, to let them know . . . and for the first time, I felt relaxed. Completely relaxed. Obviously, she read it, she came, and she convinced me to go to the hospital . . . Once we got there, I was like, 'I'm not talking to anyone who's not my doctor.' So the director went in, talked to the nurses, talked to a psychiatrist . . . and then they walked in and talked to me. And then there was the first turning point in all of this.
>
> The director said, 'You have two [options], and you can choose.' One was to go home, and do what [I planned] to do. The other was to let others help me, and stay in the hospital. Even though I know now that sense of liberty was not real – she was probably going to call the police if I went home – in that moment, it felt right. I felt I had a choice, and I chose to live. To stay in the hospital. This is what I was looking for, really. I didn't want to kill myself. I was allowed to realise, to decide, I wanted my normal life back.

DM shared that, thanks to this turning point, she grasped a skillset that she never realised she had. Ever since, she has continued to apply it as needed.

> Now I know that I have in my power the ability to detect when things are going wrong, when things aren't working, and to

> decide to seek help. And I know that the help will be a relief. I know what help I need and how to ask for it.

HE, aged twenty-six (USA)

HE had struggled with overpowering emotions for as long as she could remember: 'I think I first noticed it when I was very young, six or seven. I was just a very angry kid, pretty rebellious, I got in trouble a lot [at] school for purposely misbehaving. At the time, I didn't understand where it was coming from or why.'

A few years later, her anger took a new shape – sadness and depression – that left her with the sense that she was 'just this really sad person'. She saw the sadness as a flaw, not an addressable struggle. This sense went unchecked for years, and in college, it finally reached a breaking point. She recalled one night in particular, when her distress felt uniquely overwhelming: 'There was so much of wanting all those years of pain and suffering to end . . . and feeling like the only thing I could possibly do was stop existing.'

It was that night that she planned to attempt suicide, and it was that night she realised – in an instant, and with total clarity – that maybe, life could offer more:

> It's just so vivid. Having thoughts of, 'I want more,' and 'There's got to be a way to [hold] some of this sadness, and everything that's happened to me, and to still do some of these important things in the future.'

HE stopped what she had planned to do that night, took a shower, and went to sleep. And the next day was stunningly normal. And that normality, in contrast to the night before, led to HE's turning point:

> I woke up the next day and went right to class. I think I had an exam. I just . . . carried on . . . I realised, if that [sense of sadness] can be there and I can still be here, I *must* be able to continue on. There must be a reason to keep going and doing stuff that matters to me.

Years after this experience, HE learned about the 'bus driver metaphor', which is commonly used in a form of mental health treatment called acceptance and commitment therapy (ACT). This metaphor gave her the language she needed to grasp the fuller meaning of her turning point, and to express for the first time why it had made such a difference:

> The biggest one that did that for me was the famous metaphor of driving a bus, and having your thoughts and hard experiences on the bus as passengers. You want to be the driver of your own bus. You don't want to let *them* drive it. There were so many times . . . when I wasn't driving my own bus, when I was angry or acting out, or ruining relationships because I was upset, doing things I'm not proud of, because I was letting my hard emotions and experiences take the lead . . . After getting up the next day, I was much more able to say, 'These things can be here, but they aren't driving the

> bus anymore.' So, that particular metaphor really resonated with me.

HE shared how her turning point – realising, 'If that [sense of sadness] can be there and I can still be here, I *must* be able to continue on' – helped the idea of 'driving her own bus' shift from impossible to attainable:

> In some ways, [it was the fact] that I got up the next morning . . . and took the exam – just the fact that I actually *did* that. I finished that year. I got a summer job. Throughout the next six months, I realised that I was continuing to do these things that were important to me – and I realised that in doing so, I was also feeling better in some ways. It wasn't necessarily my goal to do those things in order to feel better. But it was a by-product, a side effect of doing those things that were important to me. So I obviously didn't have the language at that time to say, 'Oh, *I'm* driving the bus now,' but I can look back [now] and see myself doing that after such a traumatic event. I know that it's something I can do. I can make that choice. It's not always an easy choice, but I can make it if I want to and [if] I'm intentional about it.

This realisation and newfound motivation also led HE to explore other aspects of herself, including her own identities and their intersections – something she had never taken the time to do. This process further solidified her will to keep going, and ultimately, to be there for others whose struggles mirrored her own.

> I took a lot of feminist and queer theory classes and [learned] a lot about my own self-identity, and the history of racism in this country . . . I'm a person of colour, and my experience in the world is different than being white. So, a lot of that self-discovery happened after the attempt. And I realised that people hadn't ever really understood me before . . . I now know that things that have happened to me have been at the intersection of racism and sexism and homophobia – not just that people had been mean to me, but it could have been due to any number of things. It made me reflect on things in a whole different way, [and see] opportunities I'd been passed over for in a new light.
>
> Now, my whole research programme is designed around making sure our work reflects the needs of marginalised populations. I don't think any of that would have been the case if I had not had my own experiences of mental health and trauma, and all that. I understood that the systems . . . hadn't worked for me, so I want to be able to help make them work better for other people.

I then asked HE, out of curiosity, 'Do you think turning points like these happen for everyone? Or do you think experiences like these are unique to your journey?'

Her response resonated deeply:

> I think they're probably *there*, but it would take some level of noticing to see them and respond to them in a way that makes them have an impact. I'm imagining a literal turning point in a road – if you're not paying attention, you can just keep

driving, but if you're looking for it, you can see the turn-off, and you can go in a different direction. So part of it might be showing up, paying attention. And there are many reasons why somebody might not be able to do that – it depends on the context. But I feel like the opportunities for turning points are there for everyone. Whether or not everyone is able to experience it is another question.

MW, aged sixty-six (USA), continued

Following MW's stay in a psychiatric ward, he described another realisation that allowed him to take new, and different, steps toward recovery.

> I determined that I needed to let go of drugs and alcohol. Now, I overestimated the potency of that experience of recognising the absolute necessity of [letting go of drugs and alcohol] as something that would actually keep me sober – which was a great mistake. It took me four months after they released me, a couple of stumbles and a total faceplant, and then I really realised two things with completely equal force and clarity: that I could not drink, and that I could not *not* drink. Like, those things were [both] absolutely true. Both of them at the same time. Realising that was a little like getting hit in the head with a two-by-four.
>
> [That realisation] got me to stop struggling not to be where I was. I started trying to be more devoted to where I was, [rather] than to getting to where I wasn't, or where I

> shouldn't be. Life got real granular, once I decided that I was going to stay. And from there, whatever was on my plate, I was going to clean that plate, just like my mom taught me.

That realisation got MW to start asking:

> What is the next right thing? What can I do right now that won't break anything or hurt anyone? How can I get one foot in front of the next? Which is, of course, what they were trying to teach me in the twelve-step programmes. It's not a logical thing; you have to find a way to acceptance. That, doing the next right thing – that was huge . . . [I started] solving the needs of the day . . . That's really simple stuff. And faithfully practised – that's the change agent.

Pathway five: Giving back

DM, aged thirty-two (Spain), continued

DM shared more distinct turning points than almost anyone I had the fortune of interviewing. Her last one resonated so strongly with me that I couldn't help but include it.

DM's stay at the psychiatric hospital left her with strengthened self-knowledge, a community of peers in recovery, and a confidence that she could seek and access the help she needed if her dangerous thoughts returned.

Her final turning point was by far her most public: DM decided to share her recovery journey with the world, to help others see a path to recovery themselves.

> Back when I was in school, I had a friend, and we were at a party . . . when she started telling me about her anxiety. I felt connected with her, so when I got home . . . I wrote to her. I told her about my depression. I wasn't telling people about it at the time, because I thought it might isolate me. She was moved by my story, and as it turns out, she was organising a talk series. So I told her, one of my dreams is to give a public speech and [share] my experience. And she said, 'Well, you have the chance if you want to give a five-minute talk.' With her encouragement, I actually did it! The talk was to make people realise that . . . anybody can become a patient in a mental hospital, like me. So could [you, or] anyone around you. One in four people may experience a mental health issue, I said . . . and that mean[s] one in four people is a superhero. And I revealed that I was wearing a 'Superman' shirt. And the audience started to cheer and clap – I told them to stop because I only had a couple of minutes! So, I told everyone that, ultimately, even though one in four people is a superhero, we need the other three to be [superheroes] too. I told them how meeting with the director, being able to step back and choose, saved me that night at the hospital. Anyone can be somebody else's superhero. Everyone has the power to help somebody else.

DM views this experience as key to her recovery. She still thinks back to that speech during difficult points in her journey. It helps her remember her strength.

> This was the first time I put it all together. Telling my story was a turning point. It felt like what I said mattered. In fact, I had a relapse after that. But when my psychiatrist saw my talk, he said, 'If you can give that talk in front of all those people, you can handle this too.'

AB, aged twenty-five (USA)

Two years into college, AB experienced mania for the first time in her life. She had struggled with depression before, but this was entirely different – a new, unsettling level of confusion and overwhelm. Treatment-seeking felt borderline-impossible while actively battling manic symptoms.

> It is pretty difficult to seek professional help (e.g. look up mental health professionals who are accepting patients and your insurance) while in the midst of a manic episode. It was also at the end of the semester, a time during which CAPS (Counselling & Psychological Services) is known to be overwhelmed. I knew that it could take weeks to see someone. I debated going into the emergency room, but I did not know what psych hospitalisations entailed. It was scary to not know what to do or where to go.

Eventually (and despite many more roadblocks than she should have had to face), AB was connected with care. But her path toward sustainable coping was not an easy one.

> At the beginning, I really struggled with the concept of being diagnosed with a lifelong condition and needing to be on psychiatric medications permanently. I think part of it was myself minimising the severity of my own condition ('I don't need meds; it's not that bad.'). Part of it was the stigma [associated with] medications (e.g. a psychology professor telling me that psych meds are not necessary). I had to take multiple semesters off from [my] undergrad. Being unmedicated was making it impossible to function as a student. Even with only summer classes, I found it impossible to concentrate. I was experiencing thoughts of suicide, which was incredibly distressing. I eventually came to accept that I needed to be on medication, and that it wasn't a weakness.

These foundations, and her increasing self-acceptance, made it possible for AB to experience a turning point in her journey. She began to channel her experiences toward supporting and allying with others living with bipolar disorder.

> I managed to help several others who were struggling with mood episodes and [suicidal ideation] (e.g. a childhood best friend became manic, and I managed to convince her to seek help when she was suicidal). Several people connected to my writing ([a] blog about lived experience). Realising that my writing and outreach was helping others made me feel like I could use my lived experience in a way that is a strength rather than a weakness, not something to be ashamed of or feel the need to hide.

Uplifting others helped AB realise strength that she couldn't yet see. Today, she continues to exercise this strength - and find meaning in the challenges she's faced - by writing about her lived experiences, advocating for mental health awareness, and lending peer support.

Chapter conclusion

This chapter and its stories show that turning points toward recovery can occur at any moment. They can happen in and beyond the context of mental health treatment, alone or with others, and at any point in life. They can shift mental health trajectories for people with widely ranging mental health problems and diagnoses, even those classified as 'severe' and 'chronic'. And they can *matter*, in remarkable ways, for each phase of life that comes next.

Many turning points centre on common themes: surprising yourself, feeling seen, seeing others, reclaiming your narrative and helping those facing similar challenges. All of these themes seem linked to the very capabilities that single-session interventions aim to build. Effective SSIs can help increase hope that change is always possible, along with the realisation that you already possess the abilities needed to bring about positive change in your life. Turning points are moments when people can start to realise their own strength, in a world focused squarely on their weakness. And these turning points are precisely what SSIs are best equipped to create.

In the introduction to this book, I described a turning point that I experienced on my own recovery journey. (Based on the coding system from this chapter, I would now describe that turning point as a moment of 'reclaiming my narrative' after a brief exchange with a fellow patient.) I stated then that my own turning point, or one like it, could have happened much earlier in my treatment. The narratives in this chapter, combined with the science behind SSIs, and how they help people heal, affirm that belief. SSIs are built to catalyse precisely the kinds of turning points that matter the most to people in recovery, including people with wide-ranging challenges, from diverse parts of the world.

Of course, not all of the turning points described in this chapter could be intentionally (or ethically) replicated. Likewise, not all of them could be experienced during a formal SSI. But, as one of the interviewees so elegantly stated: 'The opportunities for turning points are there for everyone. Whether or not everyone is able to experience [them] is another question.' SSIs create focused opportunities to either experience a new turning point that fosters positive change, or to *make meaning* of a turning point that has already occurred, but that you may not have stopped to consider. They offer you the time, support and space to understand your own strength, and start to apply it, in a new and unexpected way.

Everyone deserves moments that matter. In fact, many people have probably experienced such moments without noticing them. SSIs can help create these moments, bring them into focus, or both. It's worth restating that SSIs cannot and should not replace other forms of mental health treatment, and system-wide reform remains essential. At the same time – for the countless people who are struggling *right now* – an SSI could open a doorway they didn't know was there. And it is well within our reach to give many more people that opportunity.

4
Making More Moments that Matter

This is the part of the book where many authors might propose sweeping solutions to wickedly entrenched social problems. In this book's case, you might expect me to pontificate on how SSIs will rescue the mental healthcare system from itself, or how everyone will soon heal through brief but meaningful therapeutic moments, or perhaps both in combination. Apologies in advance if this is what you're expecting. Because it is very much not my intended point.

My point is that our mental healthcare infrastructure is incredibly broken; that its brokenness has deep, centuries-old roots; and that, although it is essential to move forward with large-scale systemic reforms, *many people who are struggling today still cannot access care.* Long-term solutions are sorely needed, and more immediate ones are needed, too.

My point is that many people experience meaningful moments, or turning points, that catalyse their journeys toward coping and recovery from mental illness. My point is that evidence-based SSIs can help more people cultivate and make meaning from these moments in their own lives. And because SSIs are easily scalable, or in many cases freely accessible, they circumvent typical barriers to accessing mental health support.

My point is that, if deployed very broadly, SSIs could be a cost-effective means of decreasing suffering for many.

SSIs will not eliminate all forms of mental illness, just as no single treatment approach will. But they may help fill otherwise-unfillable gaps in today's systems of care. If providing accessible, affordable SSIs reduced rates of depression even 1 per cent worldwide, that decline would be larger than any we've achieved in recent history. It would mean billions of dollars saved every year, given depression's well-known economic impacts. It would mean countless lives changed, and many saved – including the lives of those experiencing symptom relief, and the lives of the people who love them. Little interventions *can* carry big effects, and the scope of those effects may be clearest when viewed at the level of public health.

So, I won't claim in this chapter that SSIs are a panacea, because they are not. They represent one needed solution among many. But I will suggest some ideas for integrating SSIs into existing systems and structures – some easier to roll out than others – to help more people access brief, evidence-based support when they need it. I will offer thoughts on how to help more people experience and capitalise on moments that matter for their recovery. Later, I will share some activities from existing SSIs, which anyone can try themselves and any therapist can try with clients.

My greatest hope for this book is that it might serve as a turning point for those who read it. I hope it shows people who are struggling to find a therapist that the roadblocks they're facing are understood by (too) many. I hope it helps people in treatment find meaning in more moments along their recovery journeys. I hope it leads therapists to view *each individual session* with clients as a unique opportunity to spur long-term change. And I hope it allows those with the ability to change existing systems to view SSIs as a powerful piece of the puzzle.

In the spirit of these hopes, this chapter shares ideas and tools for embracing a single-session mindset, both individually and at scale. I hope they help you – whether you are seeking, receiving, providing or overseeing mental healthcare – to take a new step, however small, toward the change you wish to see.

Where and how will SSIs fit in?

SSIs have the potential to become a common-sense mental health safety net, helping fewer people than ever before fall through our system's large and numerous gaps. To meet this promise, SSIs must be embedded both within and beyond existing treatment infrastructure. To achieve this, they must be able to catch people in at least two categories:

1. People who want support, but are stuck *within* systems of mental healthcare. This includes people on months-long waiting lists, and those trying (and failing) to find providers who will accept their insurance.

2. People who want support, but are stuck *outside* systems of mental healthcare. This includes people who cannot – or feel unable to – disclose their mental health needs, and those who just don't know where or how to look for help.

Most new models of mental healthcare can capture the people stuck either within the system *or* outside of it, but rarely both groups at once. If thoughtfully deployed, SSIs could help support them all.

Catching people stuck within care systems

Teach therapists about SSIs

For SSIs to 'catch' people stuck within systems of care, a necessary initial step is for providers in those systems to learn about SSIs in the first place. Presently, single-session and one-at-a-time intervention approaches are rarely (if ever) mentioned in training programmes for psychiatrists or clinical psychologists (they certainly weren't mentioned in mine!). Some training programmes in social work and counselling offer ad hoc placements teaching brief intervention techniques, potentially including single-session supports – but even then, the exposure of trainees to this model is far from universal. As long as SSIs stay sidelined in therapist training curricula, embedding them into care systems will be an uphill battle.

Why do therapists so rarely learn about SSIs? The likeliest explanation involves theoretical biases that still dominate the field of psychotherapy – for instance, the ideas that more therapy is better therapy; that people with more severe mental health problems will always require longer-term treatment; and that change necessarily occurs over extended periods of time. In reality, the link between the severity of a client's difficulties and the length of effective treatment is not entirely clear. In a review of fifty clinical trials, SSIs were equally effective in reducing youth mental health problems *regardless* of symptom levels (e.g. youth with diagnoses versus youth with sub-clinical problems).[127] And in some studies, more sessions of therapy have been linked to *worse* clinical outcomes[128] – although this trend might reflect the fact that people in longer-term treatments tend to have complex and evolving mental health concerns, and they may face more obstacles to recovery regardless of treatment length. In any case, therapists-in-training deserve access to *all* of the research and clinical advances that could help them better serve their clients – including (and perhaps especially) those that challenge long-standing professional assumptions.

This could be a straightforward fix. Across therapy disciplines (social work, clinical and counselling psychology, psychiatry, marriage and family therapy, counselling), therapists-in-training should be required to learn the basics of single-session approaches: that they have existed for decades; that they can work; and that they address the unignorable reality that many clients *do* access just one session. This alone would be an enormous step forward. In fact, the core assumptions of a single-session mindset could theoretically complement any type of treatment new therapists provide. Therapists trained to adopt a competency-based approach to each session; to maximise the therapeutic potential of every moment; to communicate that change can occur even in brief periods of time; and to appreciate that all clients can bring about meaningful improvements in their lives, are therapists well-prepared to provide empowering, patient-centred care.

At the end of the book, I have compiled a reading and resource list that could provide a solid introduction to SSIs, which could be included in the curricula of different training programmes (see pages 203–207). Several of these materials are open-access and freely available to trainees (and to anyone!) interested in learning about SSIs, and incorporating the approach into their training programme, course or clinical practice.

Make it easy for therapists to offer SSIs

To make a brand-new practice 'stick' in real-world settings, *knowing* the practice is rarely enough. Structures must exist to make it easy and rewarding for therapists to use SSIs in their everyday practice, across settings and with wide-ranging patients.

To borrow a concept from user experience (UX) design: if we want more clinicians to deliver SSIs, we need to reduce 'friction' in their paths from *knowing* to *doing*. Friction is anything that makes it harder to accomplish a goal. For instance, when you order a new desk with 'some assembly required', and the instructions are so convoluted that you give up before trying to build it (a purely hypothetical example that definitely didn't cause me to write most of this book from my couch) – that is friction in action. Once therapists know they would like to use SSIs in practice, there are several supports that might help them deliver an SSI more easily. Some are more complex to set up than others, but all could substantially broaden SSI access in the long term.

Make SSI materials accessible

The first step involves making materials, guides and manuals for evidence-based SSIs *readily and easily accessible.* This step feels entirely logical – but surprisingly, intervention materials are rarely provided by research teams, even when studies identify a treatment as effective. According to a review of mental health treatment trials conducted in low- and middle-income countries, only 7 per cent of research teams (two out of twenty-seven) provided access to the intervention materials needed for real-world implementation, despite the minimal cost and effort required to do so.[157]

On this front, our lab has tried to model a new path forward for resource-sharing. We maintain a website where teens (www.schleiderlab.org/yes) and caregivers (www.schleiderlab.org/empower) can anonymously complete several online SSIs, at no cost and at any time; each of our SSIs has proven acceptable and potentially helpful in clinical trials.[103, 117, 118] We also openly share all materials needed for therapists to deliver our solution-focused Single-Session Consultation (SSC) programme,[158] which our university clinic provides to clients on waiting lists for outpatient therapy. We offer pre-recorded or live training sessions, along with access to videos of 'mock-SSC' sessions, to all who are interested in providing it.

Certainly, there are more ways to make SSI materials available than offering them freely (e.g. publishing them in a reasonably priced book, as our research team aimed to do in our workbook for teenagers – and as others have done through bibliotherapy, most famously David Burns in his bestseller *Feeling Good*,[159] although this book is not intended for completion in a single sitting). But at a minimum, when guides or protocols are identified as being useful, it should be considered *ethically essential* to share materials needed for implementation. Journals that publish trials of single-session approaches, along with mental healthcare providers' professional organisations (e.g. the American Psychological Association, American Psychiatric Association and National Association of Social Workers) could affirm and enforce such a standard – which, at the time of my writing this sentence, seems not to exist at all.

Spell out paths to sustainability

A second step involves clearly outlining models of *financing* and *sustaining* single-session services, to help identify best-fit approaches for different settings. Successful implementation efforts have been detailed by many.[73, 132, 136] Here are some examples:

- **Walk-in SSI clinics in Ontario, Canada,** which are funded through a combination of provincial and municipal funding, donations and clients' employee benefits (employee assistance programmes and employee insurance benefits), allowing clients to receive a single session on a sliding scale, often with a full or partial subsidy. Clinicians are typically volunteers or trainees, including advanced graduate students training to become therapists across multiple disciplines.

- **Our single-session consultation service at Stony Brook University's Krasner Psychological Centre,** where clients pay a sliding-scale fee for their consultation (quoted at the same price as a single psychotherapy session) while on the waiting list for outpatient treatment. Clinicians include advanced graduate students, who learn to provide and receive ongoing supervision in delivering the single-session consultation as part of their clinical training.
- **Our university's Psychiatry Department outpatient service,** where single-session consultations have been embedded into general intake procedures to augment initial patient evaluations, allowing for billing through insurance. Clinicians in this setting are generally licensed psychologists.
- **A network of nine paediatric primary care clinics in New York,** where our team led an initiative to pair depression symptom screening with digital SSIs.[160] If and when children or adolescents reported elevated symptoms of depression during an annual well-visit (all patients aged eleven and over were already being screened for depression symptoms), providers were able to immediately offer them digital, free, anonymous SSIs through our open-access website, drastically reducing the usual gap between screening

and support provision. Here, SSI clinicians are not needed. Offering digital SSIs costs the clinics nothing.

There are *many* possible models for creating sustainable pipelines for offering SSIs in healthcare settings.

Top-down support for SSI scale-up

To optimise therapists' odds of successfully providing SSIs, funders and governments should provide support and incentives to encourage their implementation. The cost-effectiveness of this sort of investment is demonstrated by the shift toward walk-in SSI clinics across Ontario, Canada. In 2012, mental health professionals Jim Duvall, Karen Young and Angela Kayes-Burden published a policy paper for the Ministry of Children and Youth in Ontario: 'No more, no less: Brief mental health services for children and youth.'[139] Based on the paper's clear and thorough recommendations, services in Ontario underwent a 'system transition process' starting in 2015, which included requiring walk-in, single-session counselling clinics to be offered in children's mental health clinics in every community across Ontario.

The government's investment paid off in spades. By providing infrastructure (physical space; support staff) and implementing financial incentives for clinics to reduce waiting times and provide walk-in services, the availability of walk-in SSI clinics skyrocketed. Today, these services have supported children, adolescents, adults and families – and approximately 50 per cent of those clients have decided that, after one session, they have received all the help they needed.[59, 139, 161, 162, 163, 164] In other words: thousands of people who would have typically waited for support for weeks or months instead received help that they considered enough, precisely when they needed it most – allowing others on waiting lists for longer-term care to connect with a therapist considerably faster. In Ontario, disseminating SSIs has shown incontestable (and incredibly cost-efficient) value.

Entire mental healthcare ecosystems stand to benefit when SSIs are brought to scale. To optimise clinicians' capacities to provide them – particularly face-to-face SSIs – large-scale investment will be instrumental.

Catching people stuck outside care systems

My suggestions so far share a critical caveat: they cannot improve mental health support for people who never access healthcare systems at all. Up to 50 per cent of adults and 80 per cent of young people with mental health needs can access *no formal treatment whatsoever.* So, a viable plan for filling treatment gaps will need to extend beyond the healthcare system itself. One promising path to realising this goal involves building SSI access points into places and spaces where people *already seek and receive mental health support:* online (from web search engines to social media platforms), through schools (from elementary schools to universities), and within existing community-based support systems (mentoring programmes). If our goal is to overcome systems that prevent people from accessing support, we must embed supports where people already are.

Connecting online help-seekers to in-the-moment support

More than 5.3 billion people use the internet globally, with 27,000 people per hour newly accessing the web.[165, 166] Based on national surveys from 2021 and 2022, over 93 per cent of adults and 97 per cent of adolescents in the United States report using the internet daily.[167, 168] So it is unsurprising that the internet has become a go-to resource for mental health information and support.[169, 170] People of all ages seek out informal help and information online: in the US, two out of three adults regularly make web-based health queries, and nearly 10 per cent of Google searches relate to personal health.[171, 172, 173, 174] These searches lead people to informational sites, self-screeners for mental health problems, or communities of peers with shared mental health experiences through social media. Not only are people comfortable using the internet to learn about their mental health, but teens and young adults often *prefer* online help-seeking to in-person help-seeking.

The ubiquity of online help-seeking creates a remarkable set of opportunities. It might be simplest for me to show you what I mean.

Imagine you are lying in bed, awake. You check your phone: 3.22am. Last time you checked, it was 1.30am, and at this point you are too tired to sleep. Even if you weren't, your thoughts are far too loud. It's like they're yelling at you: *Damnit. You missed the submission deadline. You could've sworn you set a reminder. You can't even get calendar reminders right.*

A self-blame spiral feels imminent (you recognise it from last time). Your mind tries to stop it, but that only makes things worse: *You would tell anybody else to give themselves a break. Why can't you follow your own advice? Seriously, what is wrong with you?*

The cycle continues. You consider texting a friend for support, but you don't want to worry them. You're not in danger. You just don't want to sit with this alone.

You grab your phone again and run a Google search: 'need mental health support now'. The first results page lists four expensive mental health apps, two suicide hotlines, and a treatment locator tool with links to local clinics. Nothing low-cost, nothing brief, nothing for the problem at hand – and, most critically, nothing for *right now.*

But there could be.

What if science-backed, digital SSIs could be offered *precisely when people search for mental health support online?* This approach would capitalise on every facet of what SSIs do best: it would address in-the-moment needs (whatever those needs happen to be), empower individuals to self-select which supports they access (and for how long), and circumvent cost- and stigma-related barriers linked with traditional treatment. Offering digital SSIs via thoughtfully chosen online spaces could be a seamless path to addressing population-wide mental health needs, whenever and however they emerge. (A natural – and very real – concern extending from this involves quality control in any SSIs that are disseminated. This point is essential, and we'll dive into it properly soon!)

Yoking free, evidence-based, digital SSIs to mental health-related online searches is just one of many promising possibilities. Another involves partnering with one of the countless non-profit agencies that host online self-screeners on their websites, empowering visitors to understand and act on their mental health difficulties. Examples include Mental Health America (MHA) (screening.mhanational.org/screening-tools), the National Eating Disorders Association (NEDA) (www.nationaleatingdisorders.org/screening-tool), and the UK's NHS (www.nhs.uk/mental-health/self-help/guides-tools-and-activities/depression-anxiety-self-assessment-quiz). After self-screening, users typically receive a message identifying their symptom severity range, along with a list of treatment recommendations and educational materials. What users don't yet receive – but *could*, at least in theory – are links to evidence-based digital SSIs, optimised to lend immediate support for the problems that were just identified.

Mental Health America, the largest mental health patient advocacy group in the US, hosts a suite of validated mental health self-screeners. Each year, more than 5 million people use MHA's online screener, and many of them are in immediate need of support.[175] For example, of those who used the MHA's depression screener in 2020, 71 per cent had experienced thoughts of suicide or self-harm but had never accessed formal support. Screener sites see more people with unmet mental health needs than most bricks-and-mortar clinics ever could. However, online screeners do *not* boost actual access to treatment[176] – probably because their recommended services are too difficult to access. Reimagining these online screeners as pathways to free digital SSIs could allow a far greater portion of online help-seekers to access some form of support. Even if just 1 per cent of users tried a digital SSI following MHA's self-screener, that would mean 50,000 people accessed *something* (and something evidence-based, at that!) when they otherwise might have received nothing at all. Online self-screeners could be low-risk, potentially high-reward entry points for digital SSIs.

Social media websites present another opportunity to embed digital SSIs where help-seeking already occurs. In forums, posts and direct messages, social media users routinely share their mental health symptoms and experiences, including those related to depression,[177,178] eating disorders[179] and self-harm,[180,181] in order to find support from peers with shared experiences. Critically, social media users often belong to the groups that are least likely to access traditional mental health treatment (e.g. LGBTQ+ and racial/ethnic minority young people).[166,182,183] This makes social media platforms another 'best-bet' means of bridging gaps in existing avenues to care.

Despite the potential for SSI delivery through social media, popular platforms have rarely been used for this purpose.[184] However, our team did partner with Koko – a non-profit, online mental health platform – to test whether 'in-the-moment' SSIs might be helpful, and acceptable, to users of Tumblr, a popular social media platform with more than 130 million monthly active users.[105] Users searching for mental health-related topics on the platform received a direct message with links to crisis resources and SSIs, presented as Koko 'mini-courses'. Each of these three SSIs was self-guided, five to eight minutes in length, and targeted a core idea or skill (e.g. 'taking action can help improve your mood') drawn from multi-session, evidence-based therapies (e.g. behavioural activation). Not only were people very willing to try (and complete!) the SSIs, but they seemed to concretely help: Tumblr users who finished an SSI showed meaningful drops in their hopelessness and self-hate, along with increased motivation to stop self-harm.

Offering digital SSIs precisely when people need them, whether through search engines, online self-screeners, or social media sites, reflects a wealth of untapped opportunity. Yet again, SSIs would not *replace* other forms of treatment already available. They would simply increase the odds of those in need accessing something, anything, known to lend meaningful support.

Training lay health workers to provide SSIs

Lay health workers (LHWs) go by many names, from 'community health workers' to 'peer providers' to 'family navigators'. Titles aside, they are broadly defined as non-professional providers of mental health support who share lived experience with the people they serve.[185] These lived experiences may include sharing clinical diagnoses or family experiences, or coming from the same community and sharing a cultural background. Historically, LHWs have offered community-based support for medical problems, such as cancer or HIV,[186, 187, 188] resulting in improved client health, lower healthcare costs, and narrowed treatment-access disparities along racial/ethnic and socioeconomic lines.[187, 189] More recently, LHWs have also expanded mental healthcare ecosystems.[190] Even the World Health Organization's Mental Health Gap Action Programme stressed the key role of LHWs in boosting access to science-backed interventions, especially in lower-income countries where trained providers are scarcest.[191, 192]

Training LHWs to offer SSIs, in low- and high-income countries alike, seems like a natural next step. As front-line resources within their communities, LHWs are perfectly positioned to spot people who might benefit from an SSI, and to deliver SSIs at precise moments of need. One group of LHWs that may be especially helpful to engage is mentors: volunteers (either young people or adults) who serve as caring, positive role models. In 2015, the estimated number of mentors volunteering for formal mentoring programmes in the United States was 2.59 million: *twenty-five times higher* than the number of licensed psychologists in the country at that time.[193] Beyond the sheer workforce of LHWs that mentors could provide, mentors tend to work in public-sector settings – non-profit schools, and religious organisations[194] – perfectly positioning them to boost service access in high-need, low-resource communities.

For at least two reasons, mentors could be ideal SSI providers, especially for youth. First, more than 50 per cent of young people report wanting a mentor, suggesting that mentor-delivered SSIs might be easily accepted by those they are meant to support.[195] Second, mentors are far more likely than licensed psychologists to share experiences, backgrounds and cultures with those they serve: close to 50 per cent of US-based mentors are non-white,[193] but only 16 per cent of licensed psychologists are racial/ethnic minorities.[192] Because mentors often come from and live in the same communities as their mentees, mentees might be more open to trying out an SSI with a mentor than with an unfamiliar professional.[196]

School personnel, including school counsellors and nurses, teachers and college support staff, are another LHW group worth considering for SSI training. Schools have long been touted as common-sense access points for mental health support, because they are where children, teens and young adults spend most of their time. Embedding mental healthcare within educational settings helps young people access interventions 'where they are',[197] minimising logistical barriers and stigma linked to treatment-seeking in the greater community. Unsurprisingly, young people are much more likely to use mental health services provided through schools or universities than those available through speciality mental health clinics.[198]

Why train LHWs in SSIs, as opposed to other, longer-term mental health supports? Just as SSIs are easier than longer-term treatments for people to access and complete, it costs considerably less – in terms of both time and money – to train LHWs in SSIs. Often, LHWs feel ill-equipped to deliver mental health programmes without ongoing support, consultation and supervision from trained professionals.[199, 200, 201] Fortunately, the structure of SSIs all but alleviates this concern. Many digital SSIs require no training at all, and several can be completed independently by children and teens in less than one hour. So, offering LHWs access to a suite of digital SSIs, which they could flexibly offer to mentees or students, could seamlessly complement their existing tasks and goals. Other SSIs, such as our lab's single-session consultation, have been successfully delivered by early graduate students – without any prior training in delivering psychotherapy – after just ninety minutes of training from our team. Given the efficiency of training in certain SSIs, and the dramatically larger number of LHWs relative to professionally trained therapists, the possible impact of equipping LHWs with SSIs seems too great to ignore.

Quality control in scaling up SSIs

Not all single-session supports are created equal. Just as longer-term treatments carry potential to either help or harm, so do those delivered one session at a time. When scaling up SSIs within and outside of formal mental healthcare systems, two key principles will be essential for quality control.

Not everything that takes one session is an SSI

SSIs promote the mindset that change is possible at any moment, and they empower people to bring about positive change in their lives via the strengths they already possess. They also encourage individuals to choose whether or not they pursue additional support, whether through additional SSIs or higher-intensity treatments. But single-session programmes that *directly undermine* these principles carry potential to harm. One well-known example is 'critical incident stress debriefing' (CISD), a brief group-based intervention originally intended to prevent symptoms of post-traumatic stress disorder (PTSD) in adults exposed to extreme stressors.[202] CISD is provided within seventy-two hours of a trauma to *all* individuals who experienced it, often regardless of their preferences. CISD providers require people to 'process' their negative responses to the trauma. Participants are discouraged from stopping once the session has begun. CISD providers also describe, in considerable detail, all of the PTSD symptoms that participants are likely to experience. Research shows that CISD *increases* PTSD symptoms in the long term, partly by impeding natural processes of recovery.[203]

Everything about CISD runs contrary to effective SSI design. CISD undermines client autonomy instead of promoting it: people exposed to severe trauma are coerced into taking part, even when they wish not to. It forces participants to focus on deficits, distress and future damage, rather than strengths and capabilities. It opens no pathways to change, presenting PTSD as an extremely likely outcome (which research shows it is not; most people exposed to trauma actually recover without any treatment). It is fully provider-driven, with participants told precisely what to do, when and how. And it is a 'one-and-done' programme – that is, additional sessions are not offered, even for people who would like them.

Not all multi-session therapies are helpful, and not all single-session therapies are, either. Some online tools exist to help treatment-seekers identify evidence-based treatments, including the Society for a Science of Clinical Psychology's list of evidence-supported therapies (div12.org/psychological-treatments) and the Effective Child Therapy initiative's resources for families (effectivechildtherapy.org).

When planning, delivering and scaling up SSIs across contexts, groups and settings, it is critical to centre those that directly foster (rather than undermine) single-session mindsets and contexts of competence. Likewise, these attributes will be important markers for selecting SSIs for inclusion in future public repositories of evidence-based SSIs (such repositories do not yet exist outside of academic journal articles – but hopefully they will soon!).

Assess, don't assume

Across all types of mental health interventions, there is a massive, consistent gap between rates of treatment success in RCTs versus real-world mental health settings.[204, 205, 206, 207] A key driver of this gap is that RCTs tend to measure clients' progress during treatment, using well-tested rating scales – but outside of research, whether an intervention 'works' is often decided by individual therapist judgement.[204] There are many free, brief rating scales that can accurately measure clinically meaningful treatment progress, yet only 17.9 per cent of psychiatrists and 11.1 per cent of psychologists in the US measure client treatment response at all.[208, 209] When relying on clinical judgement alone, therapists detect 'deterioration' (worsening symptoms) only 21.4 per cent of the time.[207]

Given these realities, efforts to scale up SSIs must always involve outcome measurement. Brief, validated, free scales, given before and after an SSI, can gauge whether the programme has done its job – and, in turn, when and whether more support is appropriate.

In the case of SSIs, it is important to measure whether an intervention has 'worked', along the two dimensions noted in Chapter 2: first, whether the intervention is *acceptable* (whether recipients found it personally helpful, easy to access and complete, and worth recommending to others), and whether the intervention led to *improvements in clinically important outcomes* (including hope, agency, distress and mental health symptoms). On pages 204–206, you will find two scales that our lab uses to measure SSI acceptability (one scale is for digital SSIs; the other is for our single-session consultation), along with references to other brief, free scales that can be used to guide short- and longer-term assessments of SSI impacts. Clients and providers may use responses on these surveys to decide whether their SSI has been useful, and also if and when additional care is needed.

Chapter conclusion (and making moments on your own)

At their core, SSIs are tools of empowerment. Within healthcare systems that consistently undermine agency and gatekeep treatment, SSIs present an alternative model of care: one that trusts people seeking care to know what they need and allows them to access that care exactly when they need it; one that prioritises affordability and overcomes baked-in mental illness stigma; one that reminds people of the strengths they already possess to bring about change that matters to them; and one that emphasises that every moment, just like the last and the next, is a new and real opportunity for that change to begin.

I struggled with how to end this chapter. My hope is that it catalyses a new frontier in expanding and reimagining mental healthcare systems worldwide. When it comes to SSIs, there are too many points of opportunity, and too many people with unmet needs, to ethically ignore. But this ending (one of global, multi-system transformation) is inevitably far away. I'll continue to fight for it to happen, but it might still be a work in progress by the time you've read this book.

So, progress on the large-scale ending aside, I would like to provide some tools to support you in creating meaningful moments and turning points of your own. The activities on the following pages are made for you (and anyone) to try, at any time, whenever and wherever you would like. Some of them draw on evidence-backed SSIs that our research team has created; others highlight key 'turning point' themes, uncovered in the previous chapter's narratives. You may try each activity just once or many times, on your own, with a friend, or with a therapist. The same activity could lead to different ideas, emotions, and conclusions at different times. These tools are not meant to replace formal therapy. And, at the same time, meaningful change can happen at any moment, including this one.

I hope you find them helpful in finding, crafting and sharing more moments that matter.

Activities

> **NOTE:** *Versions of Activities 1, 2 and 3 have been previously published and are available freely on Open Science Framework and at www.schleiderlab.org/yes. Contents are the intellectual property of the author; they are reproduced here with her permission.*

Activity 1: Single-session (self-)consultation

Craft a plan to get one step closer to your goals.

Welcome to your single-session (self-)consultation

Many people facing difficulties with emotional health find that just one short session or activity can help quite a bit.

This activity was built to help you get a better handle on things, or at least to jump-start movement in a positive direction. It can be used just once or many times – whenever you'd like support in navigating a problem you are facing. If this sounds good to you, let's get started.

First, name your top struggle

If you were to describe a 'top struggle' you're experiencing right now, in just a sentence or two – what would it be? Try to be as specific as possible, focusing on a *feeling*, *action* or *thought* that is causing you difficulty.

Examples

- *'I feel overwhelmed with schoolwork.'*
- *'I feel disconnected from my friends.'*
- *'I worry too much about the future.'*
- *'I am mean to myself.'*

Your top struggle today: ______________________________

____

Next, name your top hope for this activity

What do you hope to feel better able to do, think or feel after this activity? Think of your top hope as a 'positive opposite' to your top struggle – a sign that your top struggle is getting just a little bit more manageable.

Examples

- *'I hope to make a plan to finish my schoolwork today.'*
- *'I hope to feel more connected to my best friend.'*
- *'I hope to practise being mindful and focusing on the here and now.'*
- *'I hope to be kind to myself today.'*

Your top hope for this activity: ______________________________

____

Now, imagine a miracle happens

Suppose that while you are sleeping, a miracle occurs. The top struggle you're facing today completely disappears. The miracle happened while you were asleep, so when you wake up, you don't realise it occurred right away.

When you wake up, how can you tell that your top struggle is completely gone?

How would your *emotions* change? ______________________________

____

How would your *self-talk* change? ______________________________

____

What would it be *easier to do?* ______________________________

____

How close to reality is your Miracle Day?

Here is a scale from one to ten. Ten means that everything you imagined about your Miracle Day is happening right now. One means that you are as far from your Miracle Day as possible.

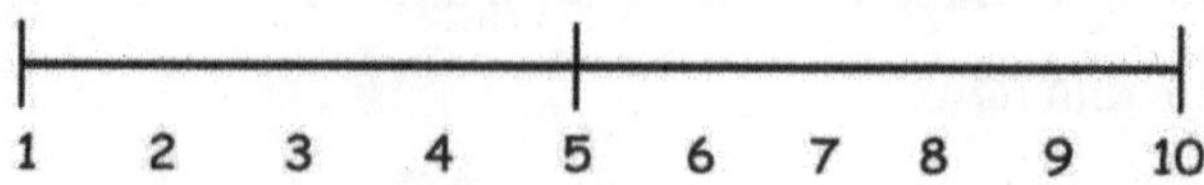

What is your rating right now? ______________________________

____

Expecting anyone to instantly get to ten out of ten on their Miracle Day scale isn't fair. So let's make an Action Plan to help you get just one point higher.

Try to name three small actions you can take to help you get one point higher on your Miracle Day scale

Here are some ideas for small actions, or you can choose your own:

- talk with a friend
- talk with a mentor
- journal
- check in with group text
- ask someone I trust for advice
- play with a pet
- exercise
- do something nice for somebody else
- play video games
- meditate
- do deep breathing
- hold an ice cube until it melts
- pray
- make art
- say something kind to myself
- take a physical step back

Action 1: ______________________________

Where will you do this?______________________

Examples: *at home, at school, at work, in the park*

When will you do this?______________________

Examples: *Before school/work, around lunch, after school/work, after dinner, before bed.*

Action 2: ______________________________

Where will you do this?______________________

When will you do this?______________________

Action 3: ______________________________

Where will you do this?______________________

When will you do this?______________________

Name at least **one person** (a friend or family member) or **resource** (a counsellor or crisis line) who you trust to help you take these actions:

____

Obstacles

Following action plans can be challenging for anyone. **What is it within you** that might hold you back from taking these steps? It could be an emotion, a belief, a bad habit, or anything else **within you.** Take a moment to think, if you need it.

What is your main inner obstacle?

____

What can you do to overcome your inner obstacle? What would be ***one*** helpful *action* you can take or *thought* you can think to overcome your inner obstacle?

Name your action or thought to overcome your inner obstacle:

____

Together, your **inner obstacle** (A) and your **helpful action or thought** (B) make up your personal **coping plan.** *If I feel/experience/think* ***(A)****, I will think/do* ***(B)****.*

Great work. Just by doing this activity, you've made a change that matters. Little by little, the actions you've planned can become a lot.

Activity 2: Learning your values

Sometimes, life can feel like it's just too much. Problems can feel like they are tornado-ing around you – too big or too many to navigate. This can leave you feeling stuck in place. You *want* something to change, but it's hard to know where or how to start.

Take a moment to reflect: What's your personal **overwhelm** rating right now, in this moment? By 'overwhelm', I mean stress, anxiety or worry – whatever negative emotions the word 'overwhelm' brings up for you. 'One' is not at all overwhelmed; 'ten' is the most overwhelmed you've ever been:

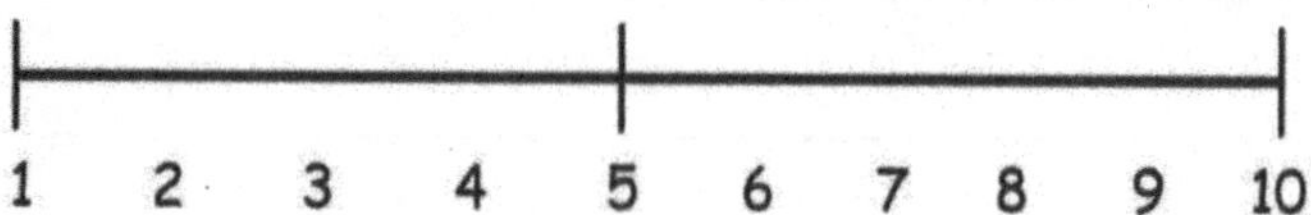

If you're at a one: That's great. Doing this ten-minute activity can help you plan for the next time your rating goes up.

If you're at a two or above: I'm sorry things are tough. Doing this ten-minute activity can help you take steps toward lowering your rating, at least a little bit.

To know where to start in managing overwhelm, your **values** can serve as a powerful guide. Values are the things that matter most to you in everyday life. They help give your life meaning and purpose. Independence, compassion, community and relationships are all examples of personal values. Your values reflect what you care about, stand for and believe in, and they differ for everyone.

When people can <u>identify</u> and <u>act on</u> their values, they feel most like their best and true selves. This can be a powerful first step toward regaining a sense of control, getting grounded and managing overwhelm in your life.

'Acting on your values' sounds deceptively easy to do. If values are so core to your identity, shouldn't acting on them be natural and effortless?

In fact, **acting on your values takes reflection, care and intent.** Allowing yourself space to learn your values, and then finding ways to act on them, can be a key step toward recentring in times of stress. It can help you focus on what really matters and help overwhelm feel a little more surmountable.

Values differ from goals in important ways. Values are directions we want to move toward. Living by your values is a lot like travelling north: regardless of how far you go, you never actually arrive. It's a direction on a compass, not a destination. You can't *succeed* or *fail* when travelling north, you can only take steps on your chosen path. Goals are what we want to *achieve* along the way. They are more like landmarks: mountains, valleys or rivers you might cross during your journey.

For example, if you care about being *compassionate* and *helping others*, that is a value you can act on every day. Acting on this value is an ongoing process; you can do it in different ways, at different moments and in different contexts. In contrast, earning a degree in Counselling or Psychology is a *goal*: something you can cross off your to-do list once it's achieved. Once you've graduated from your programme, you are done – *even* if you continue to serve and help others afterwards, professionally or otherwise. Acting on 'compassion' has no clear end. This is how you can tell it's a value, rather than a goal.

The first step toward acting on your values is figuring out what they are. Acting on your values allows you to centre and cultivate the parts of yourself that matter most to you. In moments of stress, they can point you toward your *best next step to take* toward taking control, being your true self, and managing overwhelm, one small action at a time.

Several common values are listed in the box below. Some of them probably matter more to you than others, and each value can mean different things to different people. For each of these values, first write down what that value *means* to you. Then, rate how important that value is to you – right now, in this moment – on a scale from one (not at all important) to ten (the most important).

Examples of value descriptions: 'Wisdom, Education' might mean 'reading about topics I'm interested in' to one person, and 'talking with people with life experiences that differ from my own' to another. 'Community' might mean 'spending time with family, friends and neighbours' to one person, and 'learning about my culture and family history' to another.

Any value description that feels right to you is the one you should use.

1. WELLNESS, HEALTH
   a. To you, this value means:

   ____

   b. How important is this value to you (1–10)?

   ____

2. FAMILY
   a. To you, this value means:

   ____

   b. How important is this value to you (1–10)?

   ____

3. COMPASSION, HELPING

   a. To you, this value means:

   ____

   b. How important is this value to you (1–10)?

   ____

4. WISDOM, EDUCATION

   a. To you, this value means:

   ____

   b. How important is this value to you (1–10)?

   ____

5. RELATIONSHIPS, KINSHIP

   a. To you, this value means:

   ____

   b. How important is this value to you (1–10)?

   ____

6. JOY, PLEASURE

   a. To you, this value means:

   ____

   b. How important is this value to you (1–10)?

   ____

7. SPIRITUALITY, RELIGION
   a. To you, this value means:

   ____

   b. How important is this value to you (1–10)?

   ____

8. PERSEVERANCE
   a. To you, this value means:

   ____

   b. How important is this value to you (1–10)?

   ____

9. INDEPENDENCE
   a. To you, this value means:

   ____

   b. How important is this value to you (1–10)?

   ____

10. COMMUNITY
    a. To you, this value means:

    ____

    b. How important is this value to you (1-10)?

    ____

11. ANOTHER VALUE:

____

    a. To you, this value means:

    ____

    b. How important is this value to you (1–10)?

    ____

12. ANOTHER VALUE:

____

    a. To you, this value means:

    ____

    b. How important is this value to you (1–10)?

    ____

Now, choose the **two values** that matter the most to you today. For each one, reflect on why it is important to you. Then write down something related to this value that you can do in the next twenty-four hours (your immediate goal), in the next week (your short-term goal), and in the next year or two (your long-term goal).

Value 1 _______________

What makes this value matter to you?

____

____

Your immediate goal

___

Your short-term goal

___

Your long-term goal

___

Value 2 ___

What makes this value matter to you?

___

___

Your immediate goal

___

Your short-term goal

___

Your long-term goal

___

Finally – choose *one* of these two values to focus on. Think about a specific time in your life when you got to really express or act on this value. In answering the questions that follow, include as much detail as you can.

What did you *do* to act on your value, and how did you *feel* after doing so?

___

___

What were you *thinking* about while expressing this value?

___

How did other others *react* when you acted on your value?

___

If you faced any *obstacles* to acting on your value, what were they, and how did you overcome them?

___

___

In moments of overwhelm, your answers in this activity may be your guide toward values-based action – doing more of what matters, what helps you find meaning, and what makes you feel like your best and truest self.

One last question: What's your personal **overwhelm** rating right now, in this moment?

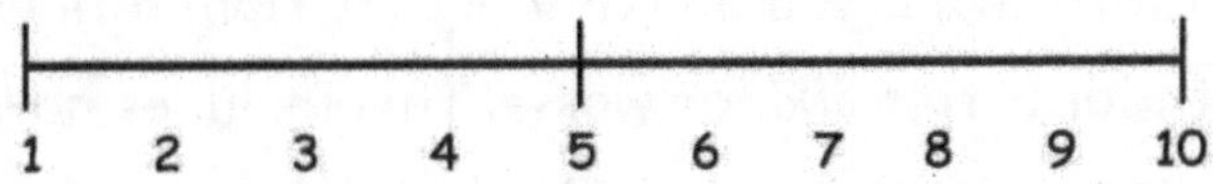

If your rating is even one point lower than when you started this activity, consider that a win. Every step forward can make a difference, no matter how small it seems.

Activity 3: Action Brings Change (ABC)

Depression and anxiety can make you feel stuck in place. This activity was designed to help you get unstuck and do more of what matters – one step at a time.

Have you ever noticed that what you do can change how you feel?

- Hearing sad music can make you cry.
- Connecting with an old friend can make you feel joyful.
- Going on a hike can make you feel energised.

Even a *very small* action – like looking at the adorable puppies and kitten on page 183 of this book – can change your mood, at least a little bit.

(If you haven't already, take a quick look at page 183!)

The change may not be big. But it's also not nothing. In our lab's research, among people who complete this activity, more than 95 per cent say that seeing cute photos of puppies and kittens makes them feel at least a *little* better. This is just one way in which what you do shapes how you feel.

Importantly, what you do (your actions) can influence your mood both for better *and* for worse. This includes how you act when dealing with stress and setbacks.

Here's an example from KP (aged twenty), who completed this activity previously:

> *I love art, maybe more than anything. And I thought I was good at it – it's what I went to school for. But in my first semester at college, I got rejected from the advanced painting seminar. It hurt so much . . . I felt so worthless. Like a failure. I honestly wanted to crawl into a hole and do nothing, talk to no one . . . honestly, that's exactly what I did for a while.*

KP's response is far from unusual. To understand why, it's helpful to consider how human brains evolved to function. Stressful events (like getting rejected from an advanced art seminar) trigger an automatic 'hide-mode' response in the human brain. This part of the brain helped early humans stay safe from very real threats (by helping us avoid getting eaten by sabretooth tigers). And sometimes, it still does protect you from danger (for instance, by urging you to keep a distance from people, places and events that really could cause harm). But at other times, our brain can **make mistakes.** It can stay in hide-mode for longer than you need it to – even after the threat, crisis or stressful event is gone.

When your brain enters hide-mode for too long, it's common to fall into a **stress spiral.** The more stress you experience, the harder it becomes to do the things you once loved – and the easier it becomes to fall into a spiral. This makes it even *more* likely that you will experience additional stress, anxiety or sadness, making it harder and harder to do anything at all.

This happens to lots of people: in fact, at some point in their lives, one out of every five people falls into a serious stress spiral lasting two weeks or longer.

Getting out of stress spirals isn't always easy, and falling into one is never your fault. And there are still **concrete steps you can take** to reverse your spiral from *sadness* to *support.*

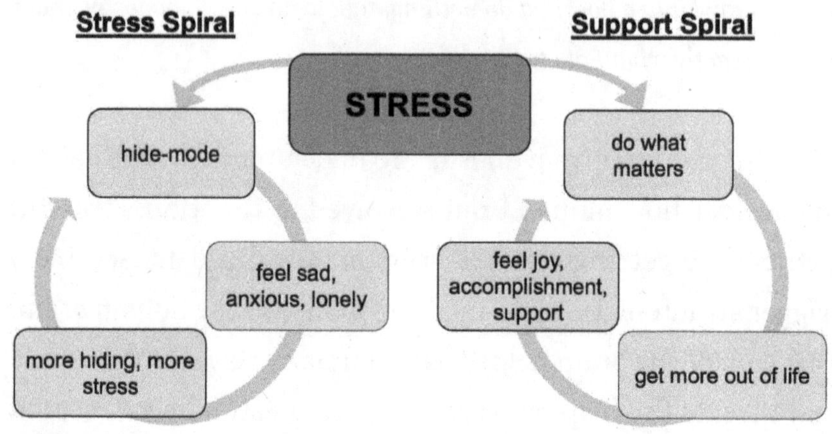

Research shows that at least three types of actions can help shift your cycle from stress to support:

Connecting with others.

Achieving goals that matter to you.

Enjoying activities on your own.

These steps can help you feel better, step by step, because they match your **current actions** to your long-term values. As we saw on page 165, values are very personal, and we never 'reach' them – we just live them through our day-to-day actions.

Acting more in line with our values is what helps us out of stress spirals.

Here is how KP used these steps to manage – and reverse – his own sadness spiral:

> *I started doing things that made me feel like myself. I focused on my photography more, just for myself. It felt good, no matter how things went. I also got back in touch with an old friend. It didn't help right away, but soon I really did start to feel better. I've even built the confidence to get back into painting.*

To help reverse your own sadness spirals in the future, you can make a plan to guide your future self – in small but meaningful ways.

First, plan a way to connect with others

Choose an activity you can do with someone you care about:

- send them a text message
- talk to them on the phone
- share a meal or snack
- do a small nice thing for them
- take a walk together
- watch a movie or a show together
- bake something together

- play a game together
- other: ______________

When will you try to make time to do this activity? (Planning a time for it can help make it happen!) Pick one:

- after getting up
- before school/work
- during lunchtime
- right after school/work
- right after dinner
- right before bed

Who would you like to do this activity with?

Second, make a plan for working toward a goal that matters to you

First, pick one big goal that feels important to you:

- do well at work or in school
- improve at a hobby
- get more physically active

If you chose 'do well at work or in school' as your big goal, select a smaller action to help you get there:

- turn in work on time
- work for ten minutes on a challenging task
- study a little each day
- get to school/work on time
- ask for help when I need it
- other: ________________________

If you chose 'improve at a hobby' as your big goal, select a smaller action to help you get there:

- spend 10 minutes on the hobby
- talk to a mentor about the hobby
- watch tutorials about the hobby
- challenge myself while doing the hobby
- other: _____________________

If you chose 'get more physically active' as your big goal, select a smaller action to help you get there:

- dance to your favourite song
- play a sport
- take a ten-minute walk
- go for a short run
- stretch for 10 minutes
- other: _____________________

When will you try to make time to do this activity? Pick one.

- after getting up
- before school/work
- during lunchtime
- right after school/work
- right after dinner
- right before bed

Third, make a plan to enjoy an activity on your own

Choose an activity from the list below (or choose your own). Try to pick something that's easy for you to do on a regular basis.

- talk with a friend
- talk with a mentor
- journal
- check in with group text
- ask someone I trust for advice
- play with a pet
- exercise
- do something nice for somebody else
- play video games
- meditate
- do deep breathing
- listen to my favourite song

- pray
- make art
- say something kind to myself
- watch my favourite show/movie

Which activity did you choose?

___

When will you try to make time to do this activity? Pick one.

- after getting up
- before school/work
- during lunchtime
- right after school/work
- right after dinner
- right before bed

Now, write in your **final Action Plan** for managing or preventing stress spirals. (Use your answers to the earlier parts of this activity to fill in the sections below.)

To connect with others, I will…

Take this small action:

___

At this time of day:

___

To work toward a goal that matters to me, I will . . .

Take this small action:

____

At this time of day:

____

To enjoy an activity on my own, I will . . .

Take this small action:

____

At this time of day:

____

My dog, Penny

Penny meeting a new puppy-friend

My cat, Mochi

Activity 4: Minding your moments that mattered

Even brief moments can have big impacts on our coping, recovery and mental health.

Take a moment to reflect on your own path toward mental health recovery and coping.

Have you had a moment when:

1. You felt *surprised* by how well you dealt with something stressful? **[Yes / No]**
2. Your problems were *seen* and *understood* by someone else? **[Yes / No]**
3. Someone else *shared some aspect of your experience* of mental health problems? **[Yes / No]**
4. You *took a new, intentional step* toward recovery? **[Yes / No]**
5. You *helped someone else* through problems similar to your own? **[Yes / No]**

Which one of these moments do you think *mattered the most* to your coping, recovery and mental health?

____

Describe the moment in as much detail as you would like:

What happened?

____

____

____

When did it happen?

____

Where were you?

____

Were you with others (and if so, who)?

____

What did you learn about yourself from this moment?

What *values* did you show in this moment? Select up to three.

- wellness, health
- family
- compassion, helping

- wisdom, education
- relationships, kinship
- joy, pleasure
- spirituality, religion
- perseverance
- independence
- community
- other: _________

What emotion did you *feel* at that moment? Select an emotion or write in your own.

- admiration
- adoration
- amusement
- anger
- anxiety
- appreciation
- awe
- awkwardness
- boredom
- empathy
- excitement
- fear
- horror
- interest
- joy

- relief
- sadness
- satisfaction
- surprise
- trust
- other: ________

What did you *think* at that moment?

____

____

Name something you *did* because of this moment. Try to choose something you wouldn't have done otherwise.

____

____

Imagine a friend is dealing with mental health difficulties that are similar to those you've experienced yourself. Based on what you learned from your own 'moment that mattered', write this friend a short letter to help them feel less alone, more understood, or more hopeful about their situation.

____

____

____

____

____

Endnotes

1 Thomas, P., Meads, G., Moustafa, A., Nazareth, I., Stange, K. C., & Donnelly Hess, G. (2008). Combined horizontal and vertical integration of care: a goal of practice-based commissioning. *Quality in Primary Care, 16*(6), 425–432.

2 Edelstein, L. (1943). *The Hippocratic Oath: text, translation and interpretation*. Baltimore: John Hopkins Press.

3 Shorter, E. (1997). *A History of Psychiatry: From the Era of the Asylum to the Age of Prozac*. New York: John Wiley & Sons, p. 33.

4 Allderidge, P. (1979). Hospitals, madhouses and asylums: cycles in the care of the insane. *The British Journal of Psychiatry, 134*(4), 321–334.

5 Shorter (2007), p. 43

6 Parry, M. (2006). Dorothea Dix. *American Journal of Public Health*, 96, 624–625.

7 Shorter (1997), p. 46

8 Bly, N. (1887). *Ten Days in a Mad House*. New York: Ian L. Munro.

9 Porter, R., & Wright, D. (Eds.). (2003). *The Confinement of the Insane: International Perspectives, 1800–1965*. Cambridge: Cambridge University Press.

10 Shorter (1997), p. 48

11 Shorter (1997), p. 68

12 Eisenberg, L., & Guttmacher, L. B. (2010). Were we all asleep at the switch? A personal reminiscence of psychiatry from 1940 to 2010 [Editorial]. *Acta Psychiatrica Scandinavica, 122*(2), 89–102.

13 Mezzina, R. (2018). Forty years of the Law 180: the aspirations of a great reform, its successes and continuing need. *Epidemiology and Psychiatric Sciences, 27*(4), 336–345.

14 Becker, T., & Vazquez-Baquero, J. L. (2001). The European perspective of psychiatric reform. *Acta Psychiatrica Scandanavia, 410 (suppl 1)*, 8–14.

15 Bolis, M. (2002). *The impact of the Caracas Declaration on the modernization of mental health legislation in Latin America and the English-speaking Caribbean*. Pan American Health Organization.

16 Fakhoury, W., & Priebe, S. (2002). The process of deinstitutionalization: an international overview. *Current Opinion in Psychiatry, 15*(2), 187–192.

17 Priebe, S., Badesconyi, A., Fioritti, A., Hansson, L., Kilian, R., Torres-Gonzales, F., ... & Wiersma, D. (2005). Reinstitutionalisation in mental healthcare: comparison of data on service provision from six European countries. *BMJ, 330*(7483), 123–126.

18 Siebenförcher, M., Fritz, F. D., Irarrázaval, M., Salcedo, A. B., Dedik, C., Orellana, A. F., ... & Mundt, A. P. (2022). Psychiatric beds and prison populations in 17 Latin American countries between 1991 and 2017: rates, trends and an inverse relationship between the two indicators. *Psychological Medicine*, *52*(5), 936–945.

19 Pew Research (2010). Prison Count 2010: State Population Declines for the First Time in 38 Years. Retrieved from: https://www.pewtrusts.org/-/media/legacy/uploadedfiles/wwwpewtrustsorg/reports/sentencing_and_corrections/prisoncount2010pdf.pdf

20 The Sentencing Project (2019). Annual Report. Retrieved from: https://www.sentencingproject.org/wp-content/uploads/2020/03/Annual-Report-2019.pdf

21 Irmiter, C., McCarthy, J. F., Barry, K. L., Soliman, S., & Blow, F. C. (2007). Reinstitutionalization following psychiatric discharge among VA patients with serious mental illness: a national longitudinal study. *Psychiatric Quarterly*, *78*(4), 279–286.

22 The Sentencing Project (2021). The Color of Justice: Racial and Ethnic Disparity in State Prisons. Retrieved from https://www.sentencingproject.org/publications/color-of-justice-racial-and-ethnic-disparity-in-state-prisons/

23 Wang, P. S., Berglund, P. A., Olfson, M., & Kessler, R. C. (2004). Delays in initial treatment contact after first onset of a mental disorder. *Health Services Research*, *39*(2), 393–416.

24 Borges, G., Wang, P. S., Medina-Mora, M. E., Lara, C., & Chiu, W. T. (2007). Delay of first treatment of mental and substance use disorders in Mexico. *American Journal of Public Health*, *97*(9), 1638–1643.

25 Lustig, S., Koenig, J., Resch, F., & Kaess, M. (2021). Help-seeking duration in adolescents with suicidal behavior and non-suicidal self-injury. *Journal of Psychiatric Research*, *140*, 60–67.

26 Patel, R., Shetty, H., Jackson, R., Broadbent, M., Stewart, R., Boydell, J., ... & Taylor, M. (2015). Delays before diagnosis and initiation of treatment in patients presenting to mental health services with bipolar disorder. *PLoS ONE*, *10*(5), e0126530.

27 Mental Health America (2020). Criminal Justice. Retrieved from: https://www.mhanational.org/issues/criminal-justice

28 Laderman, M., Dasgupta, A., Henderson, R., & Waghray, A. (2018). Tackling the mental health crisis in emergency departments: look upstream for solutions. *Health Affairs Blog*, *26*.

29 Gordon, R. (2019). *Prevention and early intervention for adults with mild to moderate depression*, Beyondblue/PolicyCommons. Retrieved from https://policycommons.net/artifacts/1610466/prevention-and-early-intervention-for-adults-with-mild-to/2300485/

30 Reinert, M. Fritze, D. & Nguyen, T. (October 2021). The State of Mental Health in America 2022. Mental Health America, Alexandria, VA.

31 America's Mental Health 2018 (2018). Retrieved from: https://www.prweb.com/releases/new_study_reveals_lack_of_access_as_root_cause_for_mental_health_crisis_in_america/prweb15828321.htm

32 Altiraifi, A., & Rapfogel, N. (2020). Mental healthcare was severely inequitable, then came the coronavirus crisis. Center for American Progress. Retrieved from: https://www.americanprogress.org/article/mental-health-care-severely-

inequitable-came-coronavirus-crisis/

33 Andrilla, C. H. A., Patterson, D. G., Garberson, L. A., Coulthard, C., & Larson, E. H. (2018). Geographic variation in the supply of selected behavioral health providers. *American Journal of Preventive Medicine, 54*(6), S19–S207.

34 Berchick, E. R., Hood, E., & Barnett, J. C. (2019). *Health insurance coverage in the United States: 2018*. Washington, DC: US Department of Commerce.

35 Kugelmass, H. (2016). 'Sorry, I'm Not Accepting New Patients' an audit study of access to mental healthcare. *Journal of Health and Social Behavior, 57*(2), 168–183.

36 American Psychological Association (2014, May 20). Few Americans aware of their rights for mental health coverage [Press release]. https://www.apa.org/news/press/releases/2014/05/mental-health-coverage

37 United States Department of Labor (2022). 2022 MHPAEA Report to Congress: Realizing Parity, Reducing Stigma, and Raising Awareness: Increasing Access to Mental Health and Substance Use Disorder Coverage. Retrieved from: https://www.dol.gov/sites/dolgov/files/EBSA/laws-and-regulations/laws/mental-health-parity/report-to-congress-2022-realizing-parity-reducing-stigma-and-raising-awareness.pdf

38 Douglas, M., Wrenn, G., Bent-Weber, S., Tonti, L., Carneal, G., Keeton, T., Grillo, J., Rachel, S., Lloyd, D., Byrd, E., Miller, B., Lang, A., Manderscheid, R., Parks, J. (2018). Evaluating State Mental Health and Addiction Parity Statutes: A Technical Report (2018). *Articles, Abstracts, and Reports*. 1095. https://digitalcommons.psjhealth.org/publications/1095

39 Bishop, T. F., Press, M. J., Keyhani, S., & Pincus, H. A. (2014). Acceptance of insurance by psychiatrists and the implications for access to mental healthcare. *JAMA Psychiatry, 71*(2), 176–181.

40 WHO World Mental Health Survey Consortium (2004). Prevalence, severity, and unmet need for treatment of mental disorders in the World Health Organization World Mental Health Surveys. *JAMA, 291*(21), 2581–2590.

41 Kessler, R. C., Chiu, W. T., Demler, O., & Walters, E. E. (2005). Prevalence, severity, and comorbidity of 12-month DSM-IV disorders in the National Comorbidity Survey Replication. *Archives of General Psychiatry, 62*(6), 617–627.

42 Kazdin, A. E. (2017). Addressing the treatment gap: A key challenge for extending evidence-based psychosocial interventions. *Behaviour Research and Therapy, 88*, 7–18.

43 Schleider, J. L., Dobias, M. L., Mullarkey, M. C., & Ollendick, T. (2021). Retiring, rethinking, and reconstructing the norm of once-weekly psychotherapy. *Administration and Policy in Mental Health and Mental Health Services Research, 48*(1), 4–8.

44 Hoge, M. A., Stuart, G. W., Morris, J., Flaherty, M. T., Paris Jr, M., & Goplerud, E. (2013). Mental health and addiction workforce development: Federal leadership is needed to address the growing crisis. *Health Affairs, 32*(11), 2005–2012.

45 Andrade, L. H., Alonso, J., Mneimneh, Z., Wells, J. E., Al-Hamzawi, A., Borges, G., ... & Kessler, R. C. (2014). Barriers to mental health treatment: results from the WHO World Mental Health surveys. *Psychological Medicine, 44*(6), 1303–1317.

46 Kazdin, A. E. (2019). Annual research review: expanding mental health services through novel models of intervention delivery. *Journal of Child Psychology and Psychiatry, 60*(4), 455–472.

47 Thornicroft, G., & Tansella, M. (2005). Growing recognition of the importance of service user involvement in mental health service planning and evaluation. *Epidemiology and Psychiatric Sciences, 14*(1), 1–3.

48 Groot, B., Haveman, A., & Abma, T. (2022). Relational, ethically sound co-production in mental healthcare research: epistemic injustice and the need for an ethics of care. *Critical Public Health, 32*(2), 230–240.

49 Proctor, E. K., Landsverk, J., Aarons, G., Chambers, D., Glisson, C., & Mittman, B. (2009). Implementation research in mental health services: an emerging science with conceptual, methodological, and training challenges. *Administration and Policy in Mental Health and Mental Health Services Research*, 36(1), 24–34.

50 Stirman, S. W., Gutner, C. A., Langdon, K., & Graham, J. R. (2016). Bridging the gap between research and practice in mental health service settings: An overview of developments in implementation theory and research. *Behavior Therapy, 47*(6), 920–936.

51 Martin, P., Murray, L. K., Darnell, D., & Dorsey, S. (2018). Transdiagnostic treatment approaches for greater public health impact: Implementing principles of evidence-based mental health interventions. *Clinical Psychology: Science and Practice, 25*(4), e12270.

52 Merikangas, K. R., He, J. P., Burstein, M., Swanson, S. A., Avenevoli, S., Cui, L., ... & Swendsen, J. (2010). Lifetime prevalence of mental disorders in US adolescents: results from the National Comorbidity Survey Replication–Adolescent Supplement (NCS-A). *Journal of the American Academy of Child & Adolescent Psychiatry, 49*(10), 980–989.

53 Harpaz-Rotem, I., Leslie, D., & Rosenheck, R. A. (2004). Treatment retention among children entering a new episode of mental healthcare. *Psychiatric Services, 55*(9), 1022–1028.

54 Weir, S., Wills, M., Young, J., & Perlesz, A. (2008). *The implementation of single session work in community health.* The Bouverie Centre, La Trobe University, Brunswick, Australia.

55 Abel, M. R., Gilbert, R., Bianco, A., & Schleider, J. L. (2022). 2022) When is Psychotherapy Brief? Considering Sociodemographic Factors, Problem Complexity, and Problem Type in US Adolescents. *Journal of Clinical Child & Adolescent Psychology, 51*, 740–749.

56 Barrett, M. S., Chua, W. J., Crits-Christoph, P., Gibbons, M. B., & Thompson, D. (2008). Early withdrawal from mental health treatment: Implications for psychotherapy practice. *Psychotherapy: Theory, Research, Practice, Training, 45*(2), 247.

57 Olfson, M., Mojtabai, R., Sampson, N. A., Hwang, I., Druss, B., Wang, P. S., ... & Kessler, R. C. (2009). Dropout from outpatient mental healthcare in the United States. *Psychiatric Services, 60*(7), 898–907.

58 Wells, J. E., Browne, M. O., Aguilar-Gaxiola, S., Al-Hamzawi, A., Alonso, J., Angermeyer, M. C., ... & Kessler, R. C. (2013). Drop out from out-patient mental healthcare in the World Health Organization's World Mental Health Survey initiative. *The British Journal of Psychiatry, 202*(1), 42–49.

59 Silve, A., & Bobele, M. (2011). *When One Hour is All You Have.* Phoenix, AZ: Zeig, Tucker & Theisen.

60 Saucedo Ávila, M. E., Cortés Rosales, M. E., Salinas García, F., & Berlanga Cisneros, C. (1997). Frecuencia y causas de deserción de los pacientes que asisten a consulta subsecuente de la División de Servicios Clínicos del Instituto Mexicano de Psiquiatría. *Salud Mental*, 20 (suppl.), 13–18.

61 Ono, Y., Furukawa, T. A., Shimizu, E., Okamoto, Y., Nakagawa, A., Fujisawa, D., ... & Nakajima, S. (2011). Current status of research on cognitive therapy/cognitive behavior therapy in Japan. *Psychiatry and Clinical Neurosciences*, *65*(2), 121–129.

62 Bados, A., Balaguer, G., & Saldaña, C. (2007). The efficacy of cognitive-behavioral therapy and the problem of drop-out. *Journal of Clinical Psychology*, *63*(6), 585–592.

63 Bhugra, D., Tasman, A., Pathare, S., Priebe, S., Smith, S., Torous, J., ... & Ventriglio, A. (2017). The WPA-Lancet psychiatry commission on the future of psychiatry. *The Lancet Psychiatry*, *4*(10), 775–818.

64 Woltmann, E. M., & Whitley, R. (2010). Shared decision making in public mental healthcare: perspectives from consumers living with severe mental illness. *Psychiatric Rehabilitation Journal*, *34*(1), 29.

65 Schleider, J. L. (2021). Twitter post. Retrieved from: https://twitter.com/JSchleiderPhD/status/1417127993063903232

66 Radez, J., Reardon, T., Creswell, C., Lawrence, P. J., Evdoka-Burton, G., & Waite, P. (2021). Why do children and adolescents (not) seek and access professional help for their mental health problems? A systematic review of quantitative and qualitative studies. *European Child & Adolescent psychiatry*, *30*(2), 183–211.

67 Clement, S., Schauman, O., Graham, T., Maggioni, F., Evans-Lacko, S., Bezborodovs, N., ... & Thornicroft, G. (2015). What is the impact of mental health-related stigma on help-seeking? A systematic review of quantitative and qualitative studies. *Psychological Medicine*, *45*(1), 11–27.

68 Spoerl, O. H. (1975). Single session psychotherapy. *Diseases of the Nervous System*, *36*, 283–285.

69 Bloom, B. L. (1981). Focused single session therapy: Initial development and evaluation. In S. H. Budman (Ed.), *Forms of Brief Therapy*. New York: Guilford Press.

70 Talmon, M. (1990). *Single Session Therapy: Maximizing the effect of the first (and often only) therapeutic encounter.* San Francisco: Jossey-Bass.

71 Schleider, J. L., Dobias, M. L., Sung, J. Y., & Mullarkey, M. C. (2020). Future directions in single-session youth mental health interventions. *Journal of Clinical Child & Adolescent Psychology*, *49*(2), 264–278.

72 Rosenbaum, R. (2008). Psychotherapy is not short or long. *Monitor on Psychology*, *39*(7), 4, 8.

73 Cannistra, F., & Piccirilli, F. (2021). *Single-Session Therapy: Principles and Practice.* Firenze, Italy: Giunti Psychometrics.

74 Grotjahn, M. (1946). Case C. In F. Alexander, T. M. French (1946). *Psychoanalysis: Principles and Application.* New York: Ronald Press.

75 Alexander, F., & French, T. M. (1946). *Psychoanalysis: Principles and Application.* New York: Ronald Press.

76 Sarason, S. B. (1988). *The making of an American Psychologist: An autobiography.* San Francisco: Jossey-Bass, p. 320.

77 Hill, C. E., Castonguay, L. G., Farber, B. A., Knox, S., Stiles, W. B., Anderson, T., Angus, L. E., Barber, J. P., Beck, J. G., Bohart, A. C., Caspar,

F., Constantino, M. J., Elliott, R., Friedlander, M. L., Goldfried, M. R., Greenberg, L. S., Grosse Holtforth, M., Hayes, A. M., Hayes, J. A., . . . Sharpless, B. A. (2012). Corrective experiences in psychotherapy: Definitions, processes, consequences, and research directions. (p. 5). In L. G. Castonguay & C. E. Hill (Eds.), *Transformation in Psychotherapy: Corrective experiences across cognitive behavioral, humanistic, and psychodynamic approaches* (pp. 355–370). American Psychological Association.

78 Malan, D. H., Heath, E. S., Bacal, H. A., & Balfour, F. H. (1975). Psychodynamic changes in untreated neurotic patients: II. Apparently genuine improvements. *Archives of General Psychiatry, 32*(1), 110–126.

79 Hoyt, M. F. (2009) *Brief Psychotherapies: Principles and Practices.* Phoenix, AZ: Zeig, Tucker & Theisen.

80 Talmon, 1993

81 Talmon, 1990

82 Hoyt, M.F., Rosenbaum, R., & Talmon, M. (1992). Planned single-session psychotherapy. In S. H. Budman, M. F. Hoyt, & S. Friedman (Eds.), *The First Session in Brief Therapy* (pp. 59–86). New York: Guilford Press.

83 Thompson-Hollands, J., Marx, B. P., & Sloan, D. M. (2019). Brief novel therapies for PTSD: written exposure therapy. *Current Treatment Options in Psychiatry, 6*(2), 99–106.

84 Tanner-Smith, E. E., & Lipsey, M. W. (2015). Brief alcohol interventions for adolescents and young adults: A systematic review and meta-analysis. *Journal of Substance Abuse Treatment, 51*, 1–18.

85 Öst, L. G., Brandberg, M., & Alm, T. (1997). One versus five sessions of exposure in the treatment of flying phobia. *Behaviour Research and Therapy, 35*(11), 987–996.

86 Roberge, P., Marchand, A., Reinharz, D., & Savard, P. (2008). Cognitive-behavioral treatment for panic disorder with agoraphobia: a randomized, controlled trial and cost-effectiveness analysis. *Behavior Modification, 32*(3), 333–351.

87 Edinger, J. D., Wohlgemuth, W. K., Radtke, R. A., Coffman, C. J., & Carney, C. E. (2007). Dose-response effects of cognitive-behavioral insomnia therapy: a randomized clinical trial. *Sleep, 30*(2), 203–212.

88 Deblinger, E., Mannarino, A. P., Cohen, J. A., Runyon, M. K., & Steer, R. A. (2011). Trauma-focused cognitive behavioral therapy for children: impact of the trauma narrative and treatment length. *Depression and Anxiety, 28*(1), 67–75.

89 Covi, L., Hess, J. M., Schroeder, J. R., & Preston, K. L. (2002). A dose response study of cognitive behavioral therapy in cocaine abusers. *Journal of Substance Abuse Treatment, 23*(3), 191–197.

90 Clark, D. M. (2011). Implementing NICE guidelines for the psychological treatment of depression and anxiety disorders: the IAPT experience. *International Review of Psychiatry, 23*(4), 318–327.

91 Cromarty, P., Drummond, A., Francis, T., Watson, J., & Battersby, M. (2016). NewAccess for depression and anxiety: adapting the UK improving access to psychological therapies program across Australia. *Australasian Psychiatry, 24*(5), 489–492.

92 Naeem, F., Pikard, J., Rao, S., Ayub, M., & Munshi, T. (2017). Is it possible to provide low-intensity cognitive behavioral treatment (CBT lite) in Canada without additional costs to the health system? First-year

evaluation of a pilot CBT lite program. *International Journal of Mental Health, 46*(4), 253–268.

93 Knapstad, M., Nordgreen, T., & Smith, O. R. (2018). Prompt mental healthcare, the Norwegian version of IAPT: clinical outcomes and predictors of change in a multicenter cohort study. *BMC Psychiatry, 18*(1), 1–16.

94 Cano-Vindel, A., Muñoz-Navarro, R., Moriana, J. A., Ruiz-Rodríguez, P., Medrano, L. A., & González-Blanch, C. (2021). Transdiagnostic group cognitive behavioural therapy for emotional disorders in primary care: the results of the PsicAP randomized controlled trial. *Psychological Medicine*, 1–13.

95 Kobori, O., Nakazato, M., Yoshinaga, N., Shiraishi, T., Takaoka, K., Nakagawa, A., ... & Shimizu, E. (2014). Transporting Cognitive Behavioral Therapy (CBT) and the Improving Access to Psychological Therapies (IAPT) project to Japan: preliminary observations and service evaluation in Chiba. *The Journal of Mental Health Training, Education and Practice* 9(3), 155–166.

96 Wakefield, S., Kellett, S., Simmonds-Buckley, M., Stockton, D., Bradbury, A., & Delgadillo, J. (2021). Improving Access to Psychological Therapies (IAPT) in the United Kingdom: A systematic review and meta-analysis of 10-years of practice-based evidence. *British Journal of Clinical Psychology, 60*(1), 1–37.

97 Mullin, T., Barkham, M., Mothersole, G., Bewick, B. M., & Kinder, A. (2006). Recovery and improvement benchmarks for counselling and the psychological therapies in routine primary care. *Counselling and Psychotherapy Research*, 6, 68–80.

98 Clark, D. M. (2018). Realising the mass public benefit of evidence-based psychological therapies: The IAPT program. *Annual Review of Clinical Psychology, 14*, 159.

99 Richards, D. A. , & Borglin, G. (2011). Implementation of psychological therapies for anxiety and depression in routine practice: Two-year prospective cohort study. *Journal of Affective Disorders*, 133, 51–60. 10.1016/j.jad.2011.03.024

100 Talmon, M. (2018, p. 189). The Eternal Now: On Becoming and Being a Single-Session Therapist. In Hoyt, M. F., Bobele, M., Silve, A., Young, J., & Talmon, M. *Single-Session Therapy by Walk-In or Appointment.* New York: Routledge.

101 Jones, P. J., Mair, P., Kuppens, S., & Weisz, J. R. (2019). An upper limit to youth psychotherapy benefit? A meta-analytic copula approach to psychotherapy outcomes. *Clinical Psychological Science*, 7(6), 1434–1449.

102 Miller, W. R. (2000). Rediscovering fire: small interventions, large effects. *Psychology of Addictive Behaviors, 14*(1), 6–18.

103 Sung, J. Y., Mumper, E., & Schleider, J. L. (2021). Empowering anxious parents to manage child avoidance behaviors: Randomized control trial of a single-session intervention for parental accommodation. *JMIR Mental Health*, 8(7), e29538.

104 Dobias, M. L., Schleider, J. L., Jans, L., & Fox, K. R. (2021). An online, single-session intervention for adolescent self-injurious thoughts and behaviors: Results from a randomized trial. *Behaviour Research and Therapy, 147*, 103983.

105 Dobias, M. L., Morris, R. R., & Schleider, J. L. (2022). Single-session interventions embedded within Tumblr: acceptability, feasibility, and utility study. *JMIR Formative Research*, 6(7), e39004.

106 Darnall, B. D., Roy, A., Chen, A. L.,

Ziadni, M. S., Keane, R. T., You, D. S., ... & Mackey, S. C. (2021). Comparison of a single-session pain management skills intervention with a single-session health education intervention and 8 sessions of cognitive behavioral therapy in adults with chronic low back pain: a randomized clinical trial. *JAMA Network Open*, *4*(8), e2113401-e2113401.

107 Ranney, M. L., Goldstick, J., Eisman, A., Carter, P. M., Walton, M., & Cunningham, R. M. (2017). Effects of a brief ED-based alcohol and violence intervention on depressive symptoms. *General Hospital Psychiatry*, *46*, 44–48.

108 Cartwright-Hatton, S., Ewing, D., Dash, S., Hughes, Z., Thompson, E. J., Hazell, C. M., ... & Startup, H. (2018). Preventing family transmission of anxiety: Feasibility RCT of a brief intervention for parents. *British Journal of Clinical Psychology*, *57*(3), 351–366.

109 Perkins, R., & Scarlett, G. (2008). The effectiveness of single session therapy in child and adolescent mental health. Part 2: An 18-month follow-up study. *Psychology and Psychotherapy: Theory, Research and Practice*, *81*(2), 143–156.

110 Davis, T. E., Ollendick, T. H., & Öst, L. G. (2012). *Intensive One-session Treatment of Specific Phobias*. New York: Springer.

111 Öst, L. G., Alm, T., Brandberg, M., & Breitholtz, E. (2001). One vs five sessions of exposure and five sessions of cognitive therapy in the treatment of claustrophobia. *Behaviour Research and Therapy*, *39*(2), 167–183.

112 Basoglu, M., Şalcioğlu, E., & Livanou, M. (2007). A randomized controlled study of single-session behavioural treatment of earthquake-related post-traumatic stress disorder using an earthquake simulator. *Psychological Medicine*, *37*(2), 203–213.

113 Nuthall, A., & Townend, M. (2007). CBT-based early intervention to prevent panic disorder: A pilot study. *Behavioural and Cognitive Psychotherapy*, *35*(1), 15–30.

114 Khazan, O. (August 21, 2019). The Quick Therapy That Actually Works. *The Atlantic*. Retrieved from: https://www.theatlantic.com/health/archive/2019/08/can-you-just-got-therapy-once/

115 Schleider, J., & Weisz, J. (2018). A single-session growth mindset intervention for adolescent anxiety and depression: 9-month outcomes of a randomized trial. *Journal of Child Psychology and Psychiatry*, *59* (2), 160–170.

116 Schleider, J. L., Burnette, J. L., Widman, L., Hoyt, C., & Prinstein, M. J. (2020). Randomized trial of a single-session growth mind-set intervention for rural adolescents' internalizing and externalizing problems. *Journal of Clinical Child & Adolescent Psychology*, *49*(5), 660–672.

117 Schleider, J. L., Dobias, M., Sung, J., Mumper, E., & Mullarkey, M. C. (2020). Acceptability and utility of an open-access, online single-session intervention platform for adolescent mental health. *JMIR Mental Health*, *7*(6), e20513.

118 Schleider, J. L., Mullarkey, M. C., Fox, K. R., Dobias, M. L., Shroff, A., Hart, E. A., & Roulston, C. A. (2022). A randomized trial of online single-session interventions for adolescent depression during COVID-19. *Nature Human Behaviour*, *6*(2), 258–268.

119 Osborn, T. L., Rodriguez, M., Wasil, A. R., Venturo-Conerly, K. E., Gan, J., Alemu, R. G., ... & Weisz, J. R. (2020).

Single-session digital intervention for adolescent depression, anxiety, and well-being: Outcomes of a randomized controlled trial with Kenyan adolescents. *Journal of Consulting and Clinical Psychology, 88*(7), 657–668.

120 Venturo-Conerly, K. E., Osborn, T. L., Alemu, R., Roe, E., Rodriguez, M., Gan, J., ... & Weisz, J. R. (2022). Single-session interventions for adolescent anxiety and depression symptoms in Kenya: A cluster-randomized controlled trial. *Behaviour Research and Therapy, 151*, 104040.

121 Lund, C. (2018). Improving quality of mental healthcare in low-resource settings: lessons from PRIME. *World Psychiatry, 17*(1), 47–48.

122 Ndetei, D. M., Mutiso, V., Maraj, A., Anderson, K. K., Musyimi, C., & McKenzie, K. (2016). Stigmatizing attitudes toward mental illness among primary school children in Kenya. *Social Psychiatry and Psychiatric Epidemiology, 51*(1), 73–80.

123 Campbell, A. (2012). Single-session approaches to therapy: Time to review. *Australian and New Zealand Journal of Family Therapy, 33*(1), 15–26.

124 Bertuzzi, V., Fratini, G., Tarquinio, C., Cannistrà, F., Granese, V., Giusti, E. M., ... & Pietrabissa, G. (2021). Single-Session Therapy by Appointment for the Treatment of Anxiety Disorders in Youth and Adults: A Systematic Review of the Literature. *Frontiers in Psychology, 12*, 721382.

125 Öst, L. G., & Ollendick, T. H. (2017). Brief, intensive and concentrated cognitive behavioral treatments for anxiety disorders in children: A systematic review and meta-analysis. *Behaviour Research and Therapy, 97*, 134–145.

126 Stoll, R. D., Pina, A. A., & Schleider, J. (2020). Brief, non-pharmacological, interventions for pediatric anxiety: Meta-analysis and evidence base status. *Journal of Clinical Child & Adolescent Psychology, 49*(4), 435–459.

127 Schleider, J. L., & Weisz, J. R. (2017). Little treatments, promising effects? Meta-analysis of single-session interventions for youth psychiatric problems. *Journal of the American Academy of Child & Adolescent Psychiatry, 56*(2), 107–115.

128 Weisz, J. R., Kuppens, S., Ng, M. Y., Eckshtain, D., Ugueto, A. M., Vaughn-Coaxum, R., ... & Fordwood, S. R. (2017). What five decades of research tells us about the effects of youth psychological therapy: A multilevel meta-analysis and implications for science and practice. *American Psychologist, 72*(2), 79–117.

129 Cannistrà, F., Piccirilli, F., Paolo D'Alia, P., Giannetti, A., Piva, L., Gobbato, F., ... & Pietrabissa, G. (2020). Examining the incidence and clients' experiences of single session therapy in Italy: a feasibility study. *Australian and New Zealand Journal of Family Therapy, 41*(3), 271–282.

130 Westmacott, R. (2011). *Reasons for Terminating Psychotherapy: Client and therapist perspectives*. University of Ottawa (Canada).

131 Westmacott, R., & Hunsley, J. (2010). Reasons for terminating psychotherapy: A general population study. *Journal of Clinical Psychology, 66*(9), 965–977.

132 Sung, J., Bugatti, M., Vivian, D., & Schleider, J. L. (2022, July 10). Evaluating a Telehealth Single-Session Consultation Service for Clients on Psychotherapy Wait-Lists. https://doi.org/10.31234/osf.io/k7u4r

133 Schleider, J. L., Sung, J. Y., Bianco, A., Gonzalez, A., Vivian, D., & Mullarkey, M. C. (2021). Open Pilot Trial of a Single-Session Consultation Service for Clients on Psychotherapy

Wait-Lists. *The Behavior Therapist, 44*(1), 8–15.

134 Schleider, J. L., Mullarkey, M. C., & Weisz, J. R. (2019). Virtual reality and web-based growth mindset interventions for adolescent depression: protocol for a three-arm randomized trial. *JMIR Research Protocols, 8*(7), e13368.

135 Mullarkey, M., Dobias, M., Sung, J., Ahuvia, I., Shumake, J., Beevers, C., & Schleider, J. (2022). Web-Based Single Session Intervention for Perceived Control Over Anxiety During COVID-19: Randomized Controlled Trial. *JMIR Mental Health, 9*(4), e33473.

136 Hoyt, M. F., Bobele, M., Silve, A., Young, J., & Talmon, M. (2018, p. 28). Chapter 1: Single-session/one-at-a-time walk-in therapy. In *Single-session Therapy by Walk-in or Appointment* (pp. 40–58). Routledge.

137 Slive, A., & Bobele, M. (2011). Making a difference in fifty minutes: A framework for walk-in counseling. In A. Slive & M. Bobele (Eds.), *When One Hour is All You Have: Effective therapy for walk-in clients* (pp. 37–54). Phoenix, AZ: Zeig, Tucker, & Theisen.

138 Silve, A., Maclaurin, B., Oakander, M., & Anderson, J. (1995). Walk-in single-sessions: A new paradigm for service delivery. *Journal of Systemic Therapies, 14*, 3–11.

139 Duvall, J., Young, K., Kayes-Burden, A. (2012). *No more, no less: Brief mental health services for children and youth.* www.excellenceforchildandyouth.com

140 Wasil, A. R., Kacmarek, C. N., Osborn, T. L., Palermo, E. H., DeRubeis, R. J., Weisz, J. R., & Yates, B. T. (2021). Economic evaluation of an online single-session intervention for depression in Kenyan adolescents. *Journal of Consulting and Clinical Psychology, 89*(8), 657–667.

141 How Much Does Therapy Cost In 2020? (Per Session & Hour). Thervo, thervo.com/costs/how-much-does-therapy-cost

142 Talmon, M. (2014). When less is more: Maximizing the effect of the first (and often only) therapeutic encounter. In M. F. Hoyt, M. Talmon (Eds.), *Capturing the Moment: Single session therapy and walk in services.* Bethel, CT: Crown House Publishing, pp. 27–40.

143 Tang, T. Z., DeRubeis, R. J., Hollon, S. D., Amsterdam, J., & Shelton, R. (2007). Sudden gains in cognitive therapy of depression and depression relapse/recurrence. *Journal of Consulting and Clinical Psychology, 75*(3), 404–408.

144 Antichi, L., Cacciamani, A., Chelini, C., Morelli, M., Piacentini, S., & Pirillo, L. G. (2022). Expectations in psychotherapy: An overview. *Ricerche di Psicologia-Open Access*, (1).

145 Shen, F., Sheer, V. C., & Li, R. (2015). Impact of narratives on persuasion in health communication: A meta-analysis. *Journal of Advertising, 44*(2), 105–113.

146 Van Laer, T., Feiereisen, S., & Visconti, L. M. (2019). Storytelling in the digital era: A meta-analysis of relevant moderators of the narrative transportation effect. *Journal of Business Research, 96*, 135–146.

147 Quintero Johnson, J. M., Yilmaz, G., & Najarian, K. (2017). Optimizing the presentation of mental health information in social media: the effects of health testimonials and platform on source perceptions, message processing, and health outcomes. *Health Communication, 32*(9), 1121–1132.

148 Borah, P., & Xiao, X. (2018). The importance of 'likes': The interplay of message framing, source, and

social endorsement on credibility perceptions of health information on Facebook. *Journal of Health Communication, 23*(4), 399–411.

149 Cody, C. (2017). 'We have personal experience to share, it makes it real': Young people's views on their role in sexual violence prevention efforts. *Children and Youth Services Review, 79*, 221–227.

150 Project YES. Retrieved from: www.schleiderlab.org/yes

151 Schleider, J. L., Abel, M. R., & Weisz, J. R. (2019). Do immediate gains predict long-term symptom change? Findings from a randomized trial of a single-session intervention for youth anxiety and depression. *Child Psychiatry & Human Development, 50*(5), 868–881.

152 Corrigan, P. (2004). How stigma interferes with mental healthcare. *American Psychologist, 59*(7), 614.

153 Priebe, S., Omer, S., Giacco, D., & Slade, M. (2014). Resource-oriented therapeutic models in psychiatry: conceptual review. *The British Journal of Psychiatry, 204*(4), 256–261.

154 Ringle, V. M., Sung, J. Y., Roulston, C., & Schleider, J. L. (manuscript in preparation). Mixed-methods examination of youth-reported barriers to accessing mental health services.

155 Victor, Devendorf, Lewis, Rottenberg, Muehlenkamp, Stage, & Miller (2022). Only human: Mental-health difficulties among clinical, counseling, and school psychology faculty and trainees *Perspectives on Psychological Science, 17*(6).

156 Victor, S. E., Schleider, J. L., Ammerman, B. A., Bradford, D. E., Devendorf, A. R., Gruber, J., ... & Stage, D. R. L. (2022). Leveraging the strengths of psychologists with lived experience of psychopathology. *Perspectives on Psychological Science*, 17456916211072826.

157 Watts, S., van Ommeren, M. & Cuijpers, P (2020). Open access of psychological intervention manuals. *World Psychiatry, 19*, 251–252.

158 Schleider, J. L. (2022, July 9). Single-Session Consultation for Emotional and Behavioral Health. https://doi.org/10.17605/OSF.IO/XNZ2T

159 Burns, D. (1980). *Feeling Good: The New Mood Therapy.* New York: William Morrow and Company.

160 Schleider, J. L., Dobias, M., Fassler, J., Shroff, A., & Pati, S. (2020). Promoting Treatment Access Following Pediatric Primary Care Depression Screening: Randomized Trial of Web-Based, Single-Session Interventions for Parents and Youths. *Journal of the American Academy of Child and Adolescent Psychiatry, 59*(6), 770–773.

161 Young, J., & Rycroft, P. (2012). Single session therapy: What's in a name?. *Australian and New Zealand Journal of Family Therapy, 33*(1), 3–5.

162 Young, J., Weir, S., & Rycroft, P. (2012). Implementing single session therapy. *Australian and New Zealand Journal of Family Therapy, 33*(1), 84–97.

163 Hymmen, P., Stalker, C. A., & Cait, C. A. (2013). The case for single-session therapy: Does the empirical evidence support the increased prevalence of this service delivery model?. *Journal of Mental Health, 22*(1), 60–71.

164 Young, J. (2018). Single-Session Therapy: The Misunderstood Gift That Keeps On Giving 1. In *Single-session Therapy by Walk-in or Appointment* (pp. 40–58). Routledge.

165 Cisco Annual Internet Report (2018-2023) White Paper. (2020). Published online at cisco.com. Retrieved from: https://www.cisco.com/c/en/us/solutions/

collateral/executive-perspectives/annual-internet-report/white-paper-c11-741490.html

166 Roser, M., Ritchie, H., & Ortiz-Ospina, E. (2015). 'Internet.' Published online at OurWorldInData.org. Retrieved from: https://ourworldindata.org/internet

167 Pew Research Center (2022). Teens, Social Media, and Technology 2022. Published online at PewResearch.org. Retrieved from: https://www.pewresearch.org/internet/2022/08/10/teens-social-media-and-technology-2022

168 Pew Research Center (2021). Internet/Broadband Fact Sheet. Published online at PewResearch.org. Retrieved from: https://www.pewresearch.org/internet/fact-sheet/internet-broadband/

169 Horgan, A., & Sweeney, J. (2010). Young students' use of the Internet for mental health information and support. *Journal of Psychiatric and Mental Health Nursing*, *17*(2), 117–123.

170 Pretorius, C., Chambers, D., & Coyle, D. (2019). Young people's online help-seeking and mental health difficulties: Systematic narrative review. *Journal of Medical Internet Research*, *21*(11), e13873.

171 Chaffey, D. (2022). Search engine marketing statistics 2022. *Smart Insights*. Retrieved from: https://www.smartinsights.com/search-engine-marketing/search-engine-statistics/

172 Nuti, S. V., Wayda, B., Ranasinghe, I., Wang, S., Dreyer, R. P., Chen, S. I., et al. (2014). The Use of Google Trends in Health Care Research: A Systematic Review. *PLoS ONE*, *9*(10), e109583

173 Rawal, A. (2020). Google's new health-search engine. The Startup: Medium. Retrieved from: https://medium.com/swlh/googles-new-healthcare-data-search-engine-9e6d824b3ccd

174 Vaidyanathan, U., Sun, Y., Shekel, T., Chou, K., Galea, S., Gabrilovich, E., & Wellenius, G. A. (2022). An evaluation of Internet searches as a marker of trends in population mental health in the US. *Scientific Reports*, *12*(1), 1–9.

175 About MHA Screening [Internet]. Mental Health America. Available from: https://mhanational.org/about-mha-screening#ScreeningReportsandResearch

176 Fitzsimmons-Craft, E. E., Balantekin, K. N., Graham, A. K., Smolar, L., Park, D., Mysko, C., ... & Wilfley, D. E. (2019). Results of disseminating an online screen for eating disorders across the US: Reach, respondent characteristics, and unmet treatment need. *International Journal of Eating Disorders*, *52*(6), 721–729.

177 De Choudhury, M., Gamon, M., Counts, S., & Horvitz, E. (2013). Predicting Depression via Social Media. In: Proceedings of the Seventh International AAAI Conference on Weblogs and Social Media. Association for the Advancement of Artificial Intelligence, p. 10.

178 Andalibi, N., Ozturk, P. & Forte, A, (2017). Sensitive Self-disclosures, Responses, and Social Support on Instagram: The Case of #Depression. In: Proceedings of the 2017 ACM conference on computer supported cooperative work and social computing. *ACM Press*, pp. 1485–500. Retrieved from: http://dl.acm.org/citation.cfm?doid=2998181.2998243

179 Fitzsimmons-Craft, E. E., Krauss, M. J., Costello, S. J., Floyd, G. M., Wilfley, D. E., & Cavazos-Rehg, P. A. (2020). Adolescents and young adults engaged with pro-eating disorder social media: eating disorder and comorbid psychopathology,

healthcare utilization, treatment barriers, and opinions on harnessing technology for treatment. *Eating and Weight Disorders-Studies on Anorexia, Bulimia and Obesity*, *25*(6), 1681–1692.

180 Kruzan, K. P., Bazarova, N. N., & Whitlock, J. (2021). Investigating Self-injury Support Solicitations and Responses on a Mobile Peer Support Application. *Proceedings of the ACM on Human-Computer Interaction*, 5(CSCW2), 1–23.

181 Kruzan, K. P., Whitlock, J., & Bazarova, N. N. (2021). Examining the relationship between the use of a mobile peer-support app and self-injury outcomes: longitudinal mixed methods study. *JMIR Mental Health*, *8*(1), e21854.

182 Fish, J. N., McInroy, L. B., Paceley, M. S., Williams, N. D., Henderson, S., Levine, D. S., & Edsall, R. N. (2020). 'I'm kinda stuck at home with unsupportive parents right now': LGBTQ youths' experiences with COVID-19 and the importance of online support. *Journal of Adolescent Health*, *67*(3), 450–452.

183 McInroy, L. B., & Craig, S. L. (2015). Transgender representation in offline and online media: LGBTQ youth perspectives. *Journal of Human Behavior in the Social Environment*, *25*(6), 606–617.

184 Rideout, V., Fox, S., Peebles, A., & Robb, M. B. (2021). Coping with Covid-19: How young people use digital media to manage their mental health. San Francisco CA: Common Sense and HopeLab. Retrieved from: https://www.commonsensemedia.org/sites/default/files/research/report/2021-coping-with-covid19-full-report.pdf

185 Barnett, M. L., Luis Sanchez, B. E., Green Rosas, Y., & Broder-Fingert, S. (2021). Future directions in lay health worker involvement in children's mental health services in the US. *Journal of Clinical Child & Adolescent Psychology*, *50*(6), 966–978.

186 Ayala, G. X., Vaz, L., Earp, J. A., Elder, J. P., & Cherrington, A. (2010). Outcome effectiveness of the lay health advisor model among Latinos in the United States: an examination by role. *Health education research*, *25*(5), 815–840.

187 Katigbak, C., Van Devanter, N., Islam, N., & Trinh-Shevrin, C. (2015). Partners in health: a conceptual framework for the role of community health workers in facilitating patients' adoption of healthy behaviors. *American Journal of Public Health*, *105*(5), 872–880.

188 Landers, S., & Levinson, M. (2016). Mounting evidence of the effectiveness and versatility of community health workers. *American Journal of Public Health*, *106*(4), 591–592.

189 Kangovi, S., Mitra, N., Grande, D., Long, J. A., & Asch, D. A. (2020). Evidence-Based Community Health Worker Program Addresses Unmet Social Needs And Generates Positive Return On Investment: A return on investment analysis of a randomized controlled trial of a standardized community health worker program that addresses unmet social needs for disadvantaged individuals. *Health Affairs*, *39*(2), 207–213.

190 Barnett, M. L., Gonzalez, A., Miranda, J., Chavira, D. A., & Lau, A. S. (2018). Mobilizing community health workers to address mental health disparities for underserved populations: a systematic review. *Administration and Policy in Mental Health and Mental Health Services Research*, *45*(2), 195–211.

191 Keynejad, R., Spagnolo, J., & Thornicroft, G. (2021). WHO mental health gap action programme (mhGAP) intervention guide:

updated systematic review on evidence and impact. *Evidence-Based Mental Health*, *24*(3), 124–130.

192 Singla, D. R., Kohrt, B. A., Murray, L. K., Anand, A., Chorpita, B. F., & Patel, V. (2017). Psychological Treatments for the World: Lessons from Low- and Middle-Income Countries. *Annual Review of Clinical Psychology*, *13*, 149–181.

193 American Psychological Association. (2015). Demographics of the US psychology workforce: Findings from the American Community Survey. Washington, DC. Retrieved from: https://www.apa.org/workforce/publications/13-demographics/report.pdf

194 Garringer, M., McQuillin, S., & McDaniel, H. (2017). Examining Youth Mentoring Services across America: Findings from the 2016 National Mentoring Program Survey. MENTOR: National Mentoring Partnership. Retrieved from: https://files.eric.ed.gov/fulltext/ED605698.pdf

195 Bruce, M., & Bridgeland, J. (2014). The Mentoring Effect: Young People's Perspectives on the Outcomes and Availability of Mentoring. A Report for Mentor: The National Mentoring Partnership. Civic Enterprises. Retrieved from: https://files.eric.ed.gov/fulltext/ED558065.pdf

196 Gulliver, A., Griffiths, K. M., & Christensen, H. (2010). Perceived barriers and facilitators to mental health help-seeking in young people: a systematic review. *BMC Psychiatry*, *10*(1), 1–9.

197 Weist, M. D., Goldstein, A., Morris, L., & Bryant, T. (2003). Integrating expanded school mental health programs and school-based health centers. *Psychology in the Schools*, *40*(3), 297–308.

198 Farmer, E. M., Burns, B. J., Phillips, S. D., Angold, A., & Costello, E. J. (2003). Pathways into and through mental health services for children and adolescents. *Psychiatric Services*, *54*(1), 60–66.

199 Hung, K. J., Tomlinson, M., le Roux, I. M., Dewing, S., Chopra, M., & Tsai, A. C. (2014). Community-based prenatal screening for postpartum depression in a South African township. *International Journal of Gynecology & Obstetrics*, *126*, 74–77.

200 Javadi, D., Feldhaus, I., Mancuso, A., & Ghaffar, A. (2017). Applying systems thinking to task shifting for mental health using lay providers: A review of the evidence. *Global Mental Health*, *4*, e14.

201 Mendenhall, E., De Silva, M. J., Hanlon, C., Petersen, I., Shidhaye, R., Jordans, M., ... & Lund, C. (2014). Acceptability and feasibility of using non-specialist health workers to deliver mental healthcare: stakeholder perceptions from the PRIME district sites in Ethiopia, India, Nepal, South Africa, and Uganda. *Social Science & Medicine*, *118*, 33–42.

202 Lohr, J. M., Hooke, W., Gist, R., & Tolin, D. F. (2003). Novel and controversial treatments for trauma-related stress disorders. In S. O. Lilienfeld, S. J. Lynn, & J. M. Lohr (Eds.), *Science and Pseudoscience in Clinical Psychology* (pp. 243–272). New York: Guilford Press.

203 McNally, R. J., Bryant, R. A., & Ehlers, A. (2003). Does early psychological intervention promote recovery from posttraumatic stress? *Psychological Science in the Public Interest*, *4*(2), 45–79.

204 Fortney, J. C., Pyne, J. M., Mouden, S. B., Mittal, D., Hudson, T. J., Schroeder, G. W., ... & Rost, K. M. (2013). Practice-based versus telemedicine-based collaborative care for depression in rural

federally qualified health centers: a pragmatic randomized comparative effectiveness trial. *American Journal of Psychiatry, 170*(4), 414–425.

205 Fortney, J. C., Unützer, J., Wrenn, G., Pyne, J. M., Smith, G. R., Schoenbaum, M., & Harbin, H. T. (2017). A tipping point for measurement-based care. *Psychiatric Services, 68*(2), 179–188.

206 Miklowitz, D. J., Otto, M. W., Frank, E., Reilly-Harrington, N. A., Wisniewski, S. R., Kogan, J. N., ... & Sachs, G. S. (2007). Psychosocial treatments for bipolar depression: a 1-year randomized trial from the Systematic Treatment Enhancement Program. *Archives of General Psychiatry, 64*(4), 419–426.

207 Simon, G. E., Ludman, E. J., Bauer, M. S., Unützer, J., & Operskalski, B. (2006). Long-term effectiveness and cost of a systematic care program for bipolar disorder. *Archives of General Psychiatry, 63*(5), 500–508.

208 Hatfield, D., McCullough, L., Frantz, S. H., & Krieger, K. (2010). Do we know when our clients get worse? An investigation of therapists' ability to detect negative client change. *Clinical Psychology & Psychotherapy: An International Journal of Theory & Practice, 17*(1), 25–32.

209 Zimmerman, M., & McGlinchey, J. B. (2008). Why don't psychiatrists use scales to measure outcome when treating depressed patients? *Journal of Clinical Psychiatry, 69*(12), 1916.

Glossary

This brief glossary covers some of the key terms used in the book:

ABC Project (Action Brings Change Project)

IAPT (Improving Access to Psychological Therapies)

LHW (Lay Health Worker)

PWP (Psychological Wellbeing Practitioner)

SSI (Single Session Intervention)

RCT (Randomised Controlled Trial)

Appendix

Introduction to Single-Session Interventions (SSIs): A Reading & Resource List

Abramson, A. (2022). 'More growth for patients in less time.' *Monitor on Psychology*, *53*(3), 58.

Hoyt, M. & Cannistrà, F. (2021). 'Common Errors in Single-Session Therapy'. *Journal of Systemic Therapies 40*(3).

Schleider, J. L., *et al.* (2020). 'Future directions in single-session youth mental health interventions'. *Journal of Clinical Child and Adolescent Psychology*, *49*(2), 264–278.

Schleider, J. L., *et al.* (2022). 'A randomized trial of online single-session interventions for adolescent depression during COVID-19'. *Nature and Human Behavior*, *6*, 258–268.

Hoyt, M., and Talmon, M. (eds). (2014). *Capturing the Moment: Single session therapy and walk-in services*. Bethel, CT: Crown House Publishing.

'Single session thinking'. La Trobe University, latrobe.edu.au.

Dryden, W. (2021). 'Single session therapy (on-demand webinar)'. Essential Therapy Training, essentialtherapytraining.com.

'Introducing single-session/walk-in therapy: An emergent form of service delivery (on-demand webinar)'. (2021). American Psychological Assocation, apa.org.

Dryden, W. (2018). *Single-Session Therapy (SST): 100 key points and techniques*. New York: Routledge.

Hoyt, M. F., *et al.* (2018). *Single-Session Therapy by Walk-In or Appointment: Administrative, clinical, and supervisory aspects of one-at-a-time services*. New York: Routledge.

Cannistrà, F. & Piccirilli, F. (2021). *Single-Session Therapy: Principles and Practice*. Firenze: Giunti Psychometrics.

Open-access SSI materials from the Lab for Scalable Mental Health:

Project YES (for adolescents): https://www.schleiderlab.org/yes

Project EMPOWER (for caregivers of younger children): https://www.schleiderlab.org/empower

Project Restore (for LGBTQ+ young people): https://www.projectrestore.info

Single-Session Consultation (for clinicians to deliver to adolescents or adults): https://osf.io/xnz2t/

Measuring satisfaction with and acceptability of single-session interventions

These measures were developed or co-developed by the author, and they have been published previously in peer-reviewed scientific articles. They are reproduced here with permission from the authors.

I: Programme Feedback Scale

This self-report measure may be completed by someone who has just completed a digital, self-guided online single-session intervention. Each item is scored on a range from 1 ('Really Disagree') to 5 ('Really Agree'). Scores of ≥3.5 on any given item reflect acceptability on that aspect of the programme.

Instructions: Please tell us how much you agree with each statement below.

I enjoyed the activity	Really Disagree	Disagree	Neutral	Agree	Really Agree
I understood the activity	Really Disagree	Disagree	Neutral	Agree	Really Agree
The activity was easy to use	Really Disagree	Disagree	Neutral	Agree	Really Agree

I tried my hardest during the activity	Really Disagree	Disagree	Neutral	Agree	Really Agree
I think the activity would be helpful for others	Really Disagree	Disagree	Neutral	Agree	Really Agree
I would recommend the activity to a friend going through a hard time	Really Disagree	Disagree	Neutral	Agree	Really Agree
I agree with the activity's message	Really Disagree	Disagree	Neutral	Agree	Really Agree

II: Single-Session Consultation Feedback Form

For use with the Single-Session Consultation; may be adapted for use with other single-session approaches.

Instructions: We would like to hear from all who have used our consultation service. Please take a few minutes to complete this questionnaire. Your feedback will be used to help us make this service as helpful as possible!

Please circle your answer to each question.

Did you find the consultation helpful in addressing your concern(s)?	Not at all	A little	Somewhat	Mostly	Very much
Did the consultation help you develop an action plan to address your concern(s)?	Not at all	A little	Somewhat	Mostly	Very much
How hopeful are you that the action plan will be useful?	Not at all	A little	Somewhat	Mostly	Very much
How motivated do you feel to use your action plan?	Not at all	A little	Somewhat	Mostly	Very much
Would you recommend our consultation service to others?	Not at all	A little	Somewhat	Mostly	Very much

Any other comments or feedback you would like to share?

____

____

____

III: Measures to assess clinically relevant change following SSIs

The following measures may be used to assess *immediate change* from before to after a single-session intervention. If used for this purpose, it is recommended to include specific instructions for respondents: 'Please answer based on how much you agree with each statement *right now, in this moment*' to capture *in-the-moment, immediate change* in your outcome of interest.

- **Hope (4-item version of the Beck Hopelessness Scale):** Perczel Forintos, D., Rózsa, S., Pilling, J. *et al.* (2013). Proposal for a Short Version of the Beck Hopelessness Scale Based on a National Representative Survey in Hungary. *Community Mental Health Journal, 49*, 822–830. https://doi.org/10.1007/s10597-013-9619-1
- **Perceived Agency (3-item 'Pathways' subscale within the State Hope Scale):** Snyder, C. R., Sympson, S. C., Ybasco, F. C., Borders, T. F., Babyak, M. A., & Higgins, R. L. (1996). Development and validation of the State Hope Scale. *Journal of Personality and Social Psychology, 70*(2), 321–335. https://doi.org/10.1037/0022-3514.70.2.321
- **Readiness for Change (1-item Readiness Ruler):** Moyers, T. B., Martin, T., Houck, J. M., Christopher, P. J., & Tonigan, J. S. (2009). From in-session behaviors to drinking outcomes: A causal chain for motivational interviewing. *Journal of Consulting and Clinical Psychology, 77*(6), 1113–1124. https://doi.org/10.1037/a0017189. ***Access the Readiness Ruler:*** case.edu/socialwork/centerforebp/resources/readiness-ruler

The following measures may be used to assess *longer-term change* (across two or more weeks) from before to after a single-session intervention:

- **Depression symptoms in adults or adolescents (9-item Patient Health Questionnaire/PHQ):** Kroenke, K., Spitzer, R. L., & Williams, J. B. (2001). The PHQ-9: validity of a brief depression severity measure. *Journal of General Internal Medicine, 16*(9), 606–613. https://doi.org/10.1046/j.1525-1497.2001.016009606.x
- **Anxiety symptoms in adults or adolescents (7-item Generalized Anxiety Disorder/GAD scale):** Spitzer, R. L., Kroenke, K., Williams, J. B., & Löwe, B. (2006). A brief measure for assessing generalized anxiety disorder: the GAD-7. *Archives of Internal Medicine, 166*(10), 1092–1097. https://doi.org/10.1001/archinte.166.10.1092
- Access the PHQ and GAD-7 in multiple languages for free: https://www.phqscreeners.com/

Index

Index

Index